Herbert Hoover—A Bibliography

Herbert Hoover—A Bibliography
His Writings and Addresses

Compiled by
Kathleen Tracey

Hoover Institution Press
Stanford University • Stanford, California

The Hoover Institution on War, Revolution and Peace, founded at
Stanford University in 1919 by the late President Herbert Hoover,
is an interdisciplinary research center for advanced study on
domestic and international affairs in the twentieth century.
The views expressed in its publications are entirely those of
the authors and do not necessarily reflect the views of the
staff, officers, or Board of Overseers of the Hoover Institution.

Hoover Bibliographical Series 58

Contents

Foreword

The growing interest in the career and achievements of Herbert Hoover adds to our pleasure in making this record of his life's work more accessible to scholars. This bibliography consists of a thoroughly researched listing of Mr. Hoover's published writings—his books and articles, as well as his speeches and testimonies to Congressional committees. It is organized to make it easy for users to locate Mr. Hoover's statements and opinions on the wide variety of issues which attracted his attention and concern.

The bibliography reflects the extraordinary range of President Hoover's interests. The service performed by this statesman brought honor and inestimable benefits not only to his own nation but also to mankind generally. We are confident that the more widespread his work is known, the higher will be the esteem in which Herbert Hoover will be held by this and succeeding generations.

W. GLENN CAMPBELL, *Director*
Hoover Institution on War,
Revolution and Peace

Stanford University
April 1977

Preface

The purpose of this bibliography is to provide scholars, teachers, librarians, and students with a list of Herbert Hoover's published writings and addresses. The bibliography covers the period from his engineering career at the turn of the century, through his relief work during World War I, his terms as Secretary of Commerce (1921–1928), his presidency (1929–1933), and his post-presidential years as public servant and elder statesman. Among the 1,245 entries are: books; articles contributed to books, periodicals, and newspapers; testimonies and addresses; reports; and formal letters and messages published in periodicals.

In some areas selectivity was required. Only speeches that appeared in print, and only the most important reports of government and private agencies with which Mr. Hoover was associated, are included. Because of their quantity and availability elsewhere, comprehensive coverage of his presidential publications was not attempted. Excluded entirely are President Hoover's messages to Congress and his executive proclamations and orders. These are available in *The State Papers and Other Public Writings of Herbert Hoover*, edited by William Starr Myers; *Proclamations and Executive Orders, Herbert Hoover*, issued by the Office of the *Federal Register*, National Archives and Records Service; and *Public Papers of the Presidents of the United States: Herbert Hoover*, also issued by the Office of the *Federal Register*.

The bibliography is arranged by form of publication: books, collections, contributions to books, contributions to periodicals, reports, testimonies, and addresses. Within each of these categories, entries are arranged chronologically. Each entry lists the title, place of publication, publisher, and publication date. When applicable, the name of the co-author or editor is also included, as is such relevant bibliographic information as variant title or additional source material.

Identification of the addresses is by geographic locale, date, and occasionally by audience.

Citations to newspapers refer to the indexed edition.

Provided at the end of the bibliography is a combined subject and name index in which the numbers refer to entries. An author/title index to books and collections is also included.

Printed sources of information that proved useful in the compilation of the bibliography were the *National Union Catalog of Pre-1956 Imprints*, the *Catalogue of the Public Documents*, the *Congressional Record*, as well as many newspapers and periodical indexes.

The source material itself was examined principally at two libraries: the Hoover Institution on War, Revolution and Peace at Stanford University, Stanford, California, and the Herbert Hoover Presidential Library, West Branch, Iowa. Both repositories house large collections of Mr. Hoover's published addresses, letters, magazine articles, press statements, and other material.

The assistance and cooperation of the archivists and librarians at the Hoover Institution and the Hoover Presidential Library are gratefully acknowledged. Special thanks go to Mrs. Crone Kernke, Assistant Archivist at the Hoover Institution, who collected and catalogued much of Mr. Hoover's published writings and speeches at that institution. In addition, appreciation is extended to Drs. Milorad M. Drachkovitch, Robert Hessen, Vaughn D. Bornet, and Deputy Archivist Charles G. Palm, who served as consultants for this project.

Chronology

HERBERT HOOVER (1874–1964)

1874	Born, August 10, West Branch, Iowa
1895	A.B., Geology, Stanford University
1897–1914	International mining engineer
1899	Married Lou Henry (1874–1944)
1912–1962	Trustee, Stanford University
1914	Chairman, American Relief Committee
	Received first gold medal of the Mining and Metallurgical Society of America
1914–1916	Vice-president, American Institute of Mining Engineers
1914–1920	Chairman, Commission for Relief in Belgium
1917–1920	Administrator, United States Food Administration
1918–1919	Alternating chairman, Inter-Allied Food Council
	Director-general, Relief for the Allied and Associated Powers
	Member, President's Committee of Economic Advisers, Paris Peace Conference
1918–1923	Director-general, American Relief Administration
1919	Founder, Hoover War Collection (later called the Hoover Institution on War, Revolution and Peace), Stanford University
	Member and part-time chairman, Supreme Economic Council, Paris Peace Conference

1919–1920   Vice-chairman, President's Industrial Conference

1921   Member, Advisory Committee, Limitation of
            Armaments Conference

1921–1923   Director, Russian Famine Relief

1921–1928   Secretary of Commerce of the United States

            Chairman, Colorado River Commission

1922   Chairman, President's Conference on Unemployment

1922–1925   Chairman, National Radio Conferences

1922–1926   Chairman, Annual Aviation Conferences

1922–1927   Member, World War Foreign Debt Commission

1923–1938   Chairman, Rio Grande River Commission

1924–1928   Member, Federal Oil Conservation Board

1924–1928   Chairman, Committee on Coordination of Rail and
            Water Facilities

            Chairman, National Conferences on Street and
            Highway Safety

            Chairman, St. Lawrence Waterway Commission

1926   Member, Cabinet Committee on Reorganization of
            Government Departments

1927   Director, Mississippi Flood Relief

1929–1933   President of the United States

1936–1964   Chairman, Boys' Clubs of America

1939–1940   Founder, Finnish Relief Fund

1940–1942   Chairman, Committee on Food for the Small
            Democracies

1946   Initiator (through General William H. Haskell), CARE

1946–1947	Cofounder, UNICEF
	Coordinator, food supply for thirty-eight nations in the world famine of 1946–1947.
1947	Head, special mission to investigate the economy of Germany and Austria at the request of President Truman
1947–1949	Chairman, Commission on Organization of the Executive Branch of the Government
1953–1955	Chairman, Commission on Organization of the Executive Branch of the Government
1954	Chairman, mission to Germany at the request of President Eisenhower and Chancellor Adenauer
1956–1957	Honorary chairman, First Aid to Hungary
1958	United States Representative, World's Fair, Brussels
1962	Recipient of gold medal, Stanford University, fifty years as Trustee
1964	Unanimous Resolution of Appreciation, United States Congress (third such resolution during his lifetime)
	Died, October 20, New York City

by K. E. Szymanski, Detroit, Michigan: published by K. E. Szymanski and printed by Barc Brothers, 1930.

5   THE CHALLENGE TO LIBERTY. New York: Charles Scribner's Sons, 1934.

For extracts see: "The Challenge to Liberty." *Saturday Evening Post*, September 8, 1934, pp. 5–7+; "Consequences to Liberty of Regimentation." *Saturday Evening Post,* September 15, 1934, pp. 5–7+.

Later editions: Rockford, Illinois: Herbert Hoover Presidential Library Association, 1971; New York: Da Capo Press, 1973.

6   SHALL WE SEND OUR YOUTH TO WAR? New York: Coward-McCann, 1939.

For extracts see: "Shall We Send Our Youth to War?" *American Magazine,* August 1939, pp. 12–13+; Same title in *Reader's Digest,* September 1939, pp. 21–25; Same title in *Addresses Upon the American Road, 1938–1940* (entry no. 28), pp. 116–128; Same title in *Shall We Send Our Boys to Foreign Wars?* (entry no. 27), pp. 5–8.

Later edition: New York: Crowell-Collier, 1939. (Published in pamphlet form.)

7   AMERICA'S FIRST CRUSADE. New York: Charles Scribner's Sons, 1942.

For extracts see: "The First American Crusade." *Saturday Evening Post*, November 1, 1941, pp. 9+; "You May be Sure I Shall Fight Shy." *Saturday Evening Post*, November 8, 1941, pp. 14+; "The Only Nation Since the Crusades That Has Fought the Battles of Other Peoples at Her Own Gigantic Loss." *Saturday Evening Post,* November 15, 1941, pp. 31+.

8   Gibson, Hugh, coauthor. THE PROBLEMS OF LASTING PEACE. Garden City, New York: Doubleday, Doran and Company, 1942.

For condensations see: The Hoover-Gibson Plan for Making Lasting Peace. Garden City, New York: Doubleday, Doran and Com-

Books

1 PRINCIPLES OF MINING: VALUATION, ORGANIZATION AND ADMINISTRATION: COPPER, GOLD, LEAD, SILVER, TIN, AND ZINC. New York: McGraw Hill Book Company, 1909.

2 Hoover, Lou Henry, joint translator. GEORGIUS AGRICOLA DE RE METALLICA. London: Mining Magazine, 1912.

Translated from the first Latin edition of 1556.

For reprints of footnotes see: "Theories of Ore Deposition Prior to the 17th Century." *Mining and Scientific Press* 105 (1912): 426–430; "Notes on the Development of Mining Law." *Engineering and Mining Journal* 94 (1912): 823–825.

Later edition: New York: Dover Press, 1950.

3 LIST OF BOOKS RELATING TO METALS. London: Printed by Crowther & Goodman, 191?.

Compiled while preparing the translation of DE RE METALLICA.

4 AMERICAN INDIVIDUALISM. Garden City, New York: Doubleday, Doran and Company, 1922.

For extracts see: "American Individualism." *Nation's Business,* January 1929, pp. 17+; February 1929, pp. 21–22+; March 1929, pp. 21–22+.

Later edition: Rockford, Illinois: Herbert Hoover Presidential Library Association, 1971.

Translations: Bulgarian translation by S. Miloshev, Sophia, Bulgaria: 1924; Japanese translation by Igawa Tadao, Tokyo: 1924; German translation, Berlin: Otto Stollberg, 1928; Polish translation

pany, 1942; *New Approaches to Lasting Peace.* Garden City, New York: Doubleday, Doran and Company, 1942.

For extracts see: "The Problems of Lasting Peace." *Reader's Digest,* August 1942, pp. 122–142; "Further New Approaches to Lasting Peace." *Collier's,* June 5, 1943, pp. 11+; June 12, 1943, pp. 15+; June 19, 1943, pp. 28+; June 26, 1943, pp. 33–36; *Further New Approaches to Lasting Peace by Hoover and Gibson: Articles Appearing in Collier's May* [sic]*–June, 1943.* New York: Vanderbilt-Jackson Typography, 1943; "Further New Approaches to Lasting Peace." In *Addresses Upon the American Road, 1941–1945* (entry no. 31), pp. 14–55.

Later editions: "The Problems of Lasting Peace." In *Prefaces to Peace: A Symposium.* Cooperatively published by Simon and Schuster, Doubleday, Doran and Company, Reynal and Hitchcock, and Columbia University Press, 1944; New York: Kraus Reprint, 1969.

9 ――――. The Basis of Lasting Peace. New York: D. Van Nostrand, 1945.

10 The Memoirs of Herbert Hoover. Three volumes. New York: Macmillan Company, 1951–1952. Volume 1: Years of Adventure, 1874–1920. Volume 2: The Cabinet and the Presidency, 1920–1933. Volume 3: The Great Depression, 1929–1941.

For extracts see: "My Boyhood Days." *Collier's,* February 17, 1951, pp. 13+; "Adventures Abroad." *Collier's,* February 24, 1951, pp. 22+; "Engineering's Golden Age." *Collier's,* March 3, 1951, pp. 30+; "I Never Wanted to See Europe Again." *Collier's,* March 10, 1951, pp. 26+; "Into the White House." *Collier's,* March 17, 1951, pp. 34+; "The Life of an Ex-president." *Collier's,* March 24, 1951, pp. 30+; "Herbert Hoover's Memoirs of Public Life." *Collier's,* August 11, 1951, pp. 13+. "Battling the Early Black Markets." *Collier's,* August 18, 1951, pp. 18+; "Food for 10,000,000." *Collier's,* August 25, 1951, pp. 22+; "Working for Woodrow Wilson." *Collier's,* September 1, 1951, pp. 26+; "Communism Erupts in Europe." *Collier's,* September 8, 1951, pp. 26+; "Advising the Big

Four." *Collier's,* September 15, 1951, pp. 26+; "Power Politics at the Peace Table." *Collier's,* September 22, 1951, pp. 26+; "Inside Harding's Cabinet." *Collier's,* September 29, 1951, pp. 34+; "Coolidge Prosperity." *Collier's,* October 6, 1951, pp. 32+; "Running Against Al Smith." *Collier's,* October 13, 1951, pp. 24+; "My White House Years." *Collier's,* April 19, 1952, pp. 15+; "Peace and Progress." *Collier's,* April 26, 1952, pp. 26+; "The Great Depression." *Collier's,* May 3, 1952, pp. 19+; "The Depression Deepens." *Collier's,* May 10, 1952, pp. 26+; "The Battle of Capitol." *Collier's,* May 17, 1952, pp. 22+; "The 1932 Campaign Against F.D.R." *Collier's,* May 24, 1952, pp. 26+; "Election Aftermath." *Collier's,* May 31, 1952, pp. 30+; "Enter Roosevelt." *Collier's,* June 7, 1952, pp. 73+; "My Boyhood Days." *Reader's Digest.* May 1951, pp. 37–42; "My Engineering Days." *Reader's Digest,* June 1951, pp. 129–144; "My Extracurricular Occupations." *Reader's Digest,* July 1951, pp. 140–146; "The First Big Game . . . Where's a Football?" In *Great Moments in Stanford Sports,* edited by Peter Grothe. Palo Alto, California: Pacific Books, 1952, p. 18; 'The Engineering Profession." *Consulting Engineer,* August 1963, p. 92; "Engineering as a Profession." In *Addresses Upon the American Road, 1950–1955* (entry no. 38), pp. 209–210.

Later edition: London: Hollis and Carter, 1952–1953.

Translation: German translation by Werner von Grunau, Mainz, Germany: Matthias Grunewald Verlag, 1951–1954.

11 THE ORDEAL OF WOODROW WILSON. New York: McGraw Hill Book Company, 1958.

For extract see: "The Ordeal of Woodrow Wilson." *American Heritage,* June 1958, pp. 65–85.

12 AN AMERICAN EPIC. Four volumes. Chicago: H. Regnery Company, 1959–1964. Volume 1: THE RELIEF OF BELGIUM AND NORTHERN FRANCE, 1914–1923. Volume 2: FAMINE IN FORTY-FIVE NATIONS, ORGANIZATION BEHIND THE FRONT, 1914–1923. Volume 3: FAMINE IN FORTY-FIVE NATIONS, THE BATTLE ON THE FRONT LINE, 1914–1923. Volume 4: THE GUNS CEASE KILLING AND THE SAVING OF LIFE FROM FAMINE BEGINS, 1939–1963.

Collections

Addresses

21 HOOVER AFTER DINNER: ADDRESSES DELIVERED BY HERBERT
    HOOVER BEFORE THE GRIDIRON CLUB OF WASHINGTON, D.C.,
    WITH OTHER INFORMAL SPEECHES. New York: Charles Scribner's
    Sons, 1933.

22 AMERICAN IDEALS AND THE NEW DEAL. Chicago: Republican
    National Committee, 1936.

23 AMERICAN IDEALS VERSUS THE NEW DEAL. New York: Scribner
    Press, 1936.

    Later edition: St. Clair Shores, Michigan: Scholarly Press, 1972.

24 ADDRESSES UPON THE AMERICAN ROAD, 1933–1938. New York:
    Charles Scribner's Sons, 1938.

25 AMERICA'S WAY FORWARD. New York: Scribner Press, 1938.

26 AMERICA'S WAY FORWARD. New York: Constitutional Publica-
    tions, 1939.

    Second edition.

27 SHALL WE SEND OUR BOYS TO FOREIGN WARS? (1939).

    Reprinted from various parts of the *Congressional Record*.

28 FURTHER ADDRESSES UPON THE AMERICAN ROAD, 1938–1940.
    New York: Charles Scribner's Sons, 1940.

    Later edition: Freeport, New York: Books for Libraries Press, 1972.

29 ADDRESSES UPON THE AMERICAN ROAD, 1940–1941. New York:
    Charles Scribner's Sons, 1941.

30 THREE ADDRESSES BY HERBERT HOOVER. Chicago: Human Events,
    1945.

31 ADDRESSES UPON THE AMERICAN ROAD, WORLD WAR II, 1941–
    1945. New York: D. Van Nostrand, 1946.

32 ADDRESSES UPON THE AMERICAN ROAD, 1945–1948. New York: D. Van Nostrand, 1949.

33 ADDRESSES UPON THE AMERICAN ROAD, 1948–1950. Stanford, California: Stanford University Press, 1951.

34 A CAUSE TO WIN: FIVE SPEECHES BY HERBERT HOOVER ON AMERICAN FOREIGN POLICY IN RELATION TO SOVIET RUSSIA. New York: A Freeman Pamphlet, 1951.

35 FORTY KEY QUESTIONS ABOUT OUR FOREIGN POLICY. Scarsdale, New York: Updegraff Press, 1952.

36 SPEECHES DELIVERED BY HONORABLE HERBERT HOOVER IN GERMANY. N.p., 1954.

37 THREE ADDRESSES BY HERBERT HOOVER IN GERMANY. N.p., 1954.

38 ADDRESSES UPON THE AMERICAN ROAD, 1950–1955. Stanford, California: Stanford University Press, 1955.

39 TWO ADDRESSES IN BRUSSELS, BELGIUM BY FORMER PRESIDENT HERBERT HOOVER DELIVERED AT THE BRUSSELS EXPOSITION ON AMERICAN DAY, JULY 4, 1958, AND BY MR. HOOVER, CHAIRMAN OF THE COMMISSION FOR THE RELIEF IN BELGIUM TO THE BELGIUM PEOPLE ON HOOVER DAY, JULY 5, 1958. Brussels, 1958.

40 ADDRESSES UPON THE AMERICAN ROAD, 1955–1960. Caldwell, Idaho: Caxton Printers, 1961.

Documentaries

41 Surface, Frank M. AMERICAN PORK PRODUCTION IN THE WORLD WAR. Chicago: A. W. Shaw Company, 1926.

42 Fisher, H. H. THE FAMINE IN SOVIET RUSSIA 1919–1923: THE

OPERATIONS OF THE AMERICAN RELIEF ADMINISTRATION. New York: Macmillan Company, 1927.

43   Surface, Frank M. THE GRAIN TRADE DURING THE WORLD WAR. New York: Macmillan Company, 1928.

44   Gay, George I., and Fisher, H. H. PUBLIC RELATIONS OF THE COMMISSION FOR RELIEF IN BELGIUM: DOCUMENTS. Two volumes. Stanford, California: Stanford University Press, 1929.

45   Myers, William Starr, editor. THE STATE PAPERS AND OTHER PUBLIC WRITINGS OF HERBERT HOOVER. Two volumes. Garden City, New York: Doubleday, Doran and Company, 1934.

Later edition: New York: Kraus Reprint, 1970.

46   Myers, William Starr, and Newton, Walter H. THE HOOVER ADMINISTRATION: A DOCUMENTED NARRATIVE. New York: Charles Scribner's Sons, 1936.

For extracts of chapters 15–19 see: "The Origins of the Banking Panic of March 4, 1933." *Saturday Evening Post,* June 8, 1935, pp. 5–7+; June 15, 1935, pp. 10–11+; June 22, 1935, pp. 16–17+; and June 29, 1935, pp. 5–7+. (Extracts reprinted in pamphlet with same title.)

Later edition: St. Clair Shores, Michigan: Scholarly Press, 1971.

47   Bane, Suda Lorena, and Lutz, Ralph Haswell, editors. THE BLOCKADE OF GERMANY AFTER THE ARMISTICE 1918–1919. Stanford, California: Stanford University Press, 1942.

48   ORGANIZATION OF AMERICAN RELIEF IN EUROPE 1918–1919. Stanford, California: Stanford University Press, 1943.

49   United States Department of the Interior, THE HOOVER DAM DOCUMENTS, by Ray Lyman Wilbur and Northcutt Ely. Washington, D.C.: Government Printing Office, 1948.

Second edition.

50 United States. Proclamations and Executive Orders, Herbert Hoover: March 4, 1929 to March 4, 1933. Two volumes. Washington, D.C.: Office of the *Federal Register*, National Archives and Records Service, 1974.

51 ———. Public Papers of the President of the United States: Herbert Hoover, 1929, 1930 and 1931. Three volumes. Washington, D.C. Office of the *Federal Register*, National Archives and Records Service, 1974 and 1976.

One volume is forthcoming.

Extracts and Quotations

52 Some Notes on the League of Nations. N.p., 1920.

53 Why We Are For Hoover. New York: Hoover National Republican Club, 1920.

54 Some Long View Policies for Improvement of the Farmer's Profit. Washington, D.C., 1925.

55 King, E. D., compiler. "High Promise for the Future." *Magazine of Wall Street* 39 (December 18, 1926): 312.

56 McCall, C.H., compiler. "Herbert Hoover and Credit." *Credit Monthly*, June 1928, p. 7.

57 "As a Man Thinks," in *This Man Hoover*, by Earl Reeves. New York: A. L. Burt Company, 1928, pp. 175–255.

58 Excerpts from Speeches and Writings of Herbert Hoover on Important Public Questions. Washington, D.C.: Hoover for President Committee, 1928.

Published in part as: "Secretary Hoover's Views on Tariff, as

Reflected in His Speeches and Writings." *Textile World*, April 14, 1928, pp. 43–44.

59 "Hoover Broadcasts on the Home." *Sunset*, February 1929, p. 23.

60 Knappen, Theodore M., compiler. "What Business May Expect from President Hoover." *Magazine of Wall Street* 43 (March 9, 1929): 813–815+.

61 Ashby, Lyle W., compiler. "President Hoover and Education: Excerpts from Various Addresses, 1923–1928." *Ohio Schools*, March 1929, p. 85.

62 "Hoover's Philosophy Stated in His Sayings." *New York Times*, January 26, 1930, section 9, paragraph 4.

63 "President's Message: Excerpts on Social Welfare." *Journal of Home Economics*, February 1930, pp. 111–114.

64 HOOVER EPIGRAMS: TERSE STATEMENTS BY THE PRESIDENT ON A VARIETY OF SUBJECTS. Washington, D.C.: Republican National Committee, 1932.

65 Wilbur, Ray Lyman, and Hyde, Arthur Mastick. THE HOOVER POLICIES. New York: Charles Scribner's Sons, 1937.

66 "Extracts from Addresses on Finnish Relief." In FURTHER ADDRESSES UPON THE AMERICAN ROAD, 1938–1940 (entry no 28), pp. 236–240.

67 "The Last Miles to Collectivism." In THE WELFARE STATE AND THE NATIONAL WELFARE: A SYMPOSIUM ON SOME OF THE THREATENING TENDENCIES OF OUR TIMES, edited by Sheldon Glueck. Cambridge, Massachusetts: Addison-Wesley Press, 1952, pp. 161–185.

68 "Remarks at Dedication of Herbert Hoover Public Schools." In ADDRESSES UPON THE AMERICAN ROAD, 1950–1955 (entry no 38), pp. 353–355.

69 Hirsh, Diane. "Herbert Hoover in His Own Words." *New York Times Magazine*, August 9, 1959, p. 16.

70 "You Have Plenty of Promise Ahead. . . ." *Seventeen*, February 1962, p. 68.

71 "The Philosophy of Herbert Hoover." *Consulting Engineer*, August 1963, pp. 93–95.

72 Nichols, William, FISHING FOR FUN AND TO WASH YOUR SOUL. New York: Random House, 1963.

For extracts see: "In Praise of Fishing." *Reader's Digest*, April 1963, pp. 243–246; "Fishing Presidents and Candidates." *Stanford Review*, May–June 1963, p. 1.

Translations: German translation by Bruno Wignam, Stuttgart, Germany: A. Muller, 1964.

73 Lochner, Louis P. "Herbert Hoover in His Own Words." *New York Times Magazine*, August 9, 1964, p. 15.

74 HERBERT HOOVER'S CHALLENGE TO AMERICA: HIS LIFE AND WORDS, by the editors of *Country Beautiful*. Editorial direction by Michael P. Dineen, edited by Robert L. Polley. Waukseka, Wisconsin: Country Beautiful Foundation, distributed by Doubleday, Doran and Company, 1965.

First edition.

Letters

75 Nichols, William, editor. ON GROWING UP: LETTERS TO AMERICAN BOYS AND GIRLS, INCLUDING THE UNCOMMON MAN AND OTHER SELECTIONS. New York: William Morrow and Company, 1962.

For extracts see: "Yours Faithfully, Herbert Hoover." *Reader's*

Digest, August 1942, pp. 111–115; "'President Hoover and His Friends." *PTA Magazine*, June 1963, p. 17.

76 O'Brien, Francis William, editor. THE HOOVER-WILSON WARTIME CORRESPONDENCE, SEPTEMBER 24, 1914, TO NOVEMBER 11, 1918. Ames, Iowa: Iowa State University Press, 1974.

Press Articles and Press Conferences

77 THE HOME FRONTS AND GLOBAL STRATEGY: SIX ARTICLES WRITTEN AT THE REQUEST OF THE UNITED PRESS, ASSOCIATED PRESS, THE NEWSPAPER ENTERPRISE ASSOCIATION, AND THE INTERNATIONAL NEWS. N.p., 1943.

Also published with same title in ADDRESSES UPON THE AMERICAN ROAD, 1941–1945 (entry no. 31), pp. 179–195.

78 SOME ADDITIONS TO THE DUMBARTON OAKS PROPOSALS. N.p., 1945.

Also published with same title in ADDRESSES UPON THE AMERICAN ROAD, 1941–1945 (entry no. 31), pp. 111–123.

79 PRESS CONFERENCES, MAY 5, 1929–MARCH 3, 1933. Wilton, Connecticut: National Micropublishing Corporation, 1933.

Contributions to Books and Pamphlets

Articles and Textual Statements

80 Five articles on mining.
Published in *The Economics of Mining*, edited by Thomas A. Rickard. New York: Hill Publishing Company, 1907.

Second edition, revised.
See entries no. 99, 200, 203, 204, and 206.

81 "Food and the War." In *The Day's Food in War and Peace*, prepared by the United States Food Admiinstration and the United States Department of Agriculture at the request of the Women's Committee of the Council of National Defense. N.p., 1918, pp. 9–13.

82 "Need of Stabilization." In *Stabilization of the Bituminous Coal Industry*, issued as a supplement to *Mining and Metallurgy*, March 1920, pp. 1–2.

83 "Trade Associations Should Stabilize Business." In *Cooperative Competitors*, pp. 5–6. New York: *New York Evening Post*, 1922.

84 "Statement of Secretary Hoover of the Department of Commerce." Published in *Conservation of Fisheries of Alaska*, pp. 3–5. Alaska Territorial Fish Commission, 1923.

85 "Fundamental Aspects of the Situation." In *Foreign Combinations to Control Prices of Raw Materials*, issued by the United States Foreign and Domestic Commerce Bureau. *Trade Information Bulletin*, no. 385, 1926, pp. 1–18.

86 "May Day—National Child Health Day—Looking Forward." In

May Day National Child Health Day 1926, p. 34. New York: American Child Health Association, 1926.

87   "Commercial Relations Between Sweden and the United States." In *Twentieth Anniversary Year Book: The Swedish Chamber of Commerce of the United States of America, May 1927*, edited by Oscar G. Marell. New York, 1927, p. 13.

88   Contribution to a discussion of New England industry. Published in *A Day in New England with Herbert Hoover*. Boston: New England Council, 1927.

89   Recollection of Theodore Roosevelt. Published in *Roosevelt as We Knew Him*, by Frederick S. Wood. Chicago: John C. Winston Company, 1927, pp. 422–423.

90   "The Larger Purpose of the Department of Commerce." In *Brief Review of Activities and Policies of the Federal Executive Departments*. Republican National Committee. Bulletin no. 6. 1928, pp. 94–129.

Also published in part as "Backing Up Business: The Larger Purposes of the Department of Commerce." *Review of Reviews* 28 (September 1928) pp. 278–283.

91   "Home Ownership." In *Better Homes Manual*, edited by Blanche Halbert. Chicago: University of Chicago Press, 1931, pp. 3–7.

92   "A Home Away from Home." In *The Unofficial Palace of New York: A Tribute to the Waldorf Astoria*, edited by Frank Crown-inshield. New York: Waldorf Astoria Corporation, 1939, p. 1.

93   "The Surrender of the Belgian Army: The Last 10 Days of the Belgian Army: What Really Happened." In *The Belgian Campaign and the Surrender of the Belgian Army, May 10–28, 1940*. New York: American Educational Foundation, 1940, pp. 7–12.

Also published as "The Surrender of the Belgian Army." In *Addresses Upon the American Road, 1940–1941* (entry no. 29), pp. 27–33.

94 "Jefferson and the Bill of Rights." In *Thomas Jefferson Then and Now, 1743–1943: A National Symposium,* edited by James W. Wise. New York: Bill of Rights Sesqui-Centennial Committee, 1943, pp. 53–57.

Also published as "Thomas Jefferson and the Bill of Rights." In *Addresses Upon the American Road, 1941–1945* (entry no. 31), pp. 382–385.

95 "Juvenile Delinquency." In *Our Teenage Boys and Girls,* by Lester D. Crow and Alice Crow. New York: McGraw Hill Book Company, 1945, pp. 313–314.

Reprinted from the *Brooklyn Eagle,* November 14, 1943.

96 "The Honorable Herbert C. Hoover, Former President of the United States." In *Peace, Progress, Prosperity: Centennial Republican National Convention, San Francisco, 1956.* N.p., 1956, pp. 23+.

97 "Herbert Hoover." In *F. W. Hirst By His Friends.* London: Oxford University Press, 1958, pp. 63–64.

Introductions and Prefatory Statements

98 Introduction to *Report Covering the Period of About Eight Months from the Inception to June 30, 1915* [of the Commission for Relief in Belgium].

See entry no. 481.

99 Introduction to *Part 2—Benevolent,* of the *First Annual Report* [of the Commission for Relief in Belgium].

See entry no. 482.

100 Preface to *The Food Problem,* by Vernon Kellogg and Alonzo E. Taylor. New York: Macmillan Company, 1917.

101 Introduction to *Women of Belgium: Turning Tragedy into Triumph,* by Charlotte Kellogg. New York: Funk and Wagnalls Company, 1917.

102 Foreword to *The Abingdon War–Food Book,* by Vernon Kellogg, John Wesley, and Charlotte Hepburn Ormond. New York: Abingdon Press, 1918.

103 Preface to *Food Guide for War Service at Home.* Prepared under direction of the United States Food Administration with cooperation of the United States Department of Agriculture and the Bureau of Education. New York: Charles Scribner's Sons, 1918.

104 Prefatory message in *Food Saving and Sharing: Telling How the Older Children of America May Help Save from Famine Their Comrades in Allied Lands Across the Sea.* Prepared under direction of the United States Food Administration with cooperation of the United States Department of Agriculture and the Bureau of Education. Garden City, New York: Doubleday, Page and Company, 1918.

105 Introduction to *The Future of German Industrial Exports: Practical Suggestions for Safeguarding the Growth of German Export Activity in the Field of Manufactures After the War,* by S. Herzog. Garden City, New York: Doubleday, Page and Company, 1918.

Translated from German by M. L. Turrentine.

106 Foreword to *America and the New Era: A Symposium on Social Reconstruction,* edited by Elisha M. Friedman. New York: E. P. Dutton and Company, 1920.

107 Foreword to *The House of the Good Neighbor,* by Esther Pohl Lovejoy. New York: Macmillan Company, 1920.

New edition.

108 *Preface to a Report of the United States Food Administration, April 1920.* Washington, D.C.: Government Printing Office, 1920.

109 Foreword to *Executive Personnel* . . . [of the Commission for Relief in Belgium].

See entry no. 492.

110 Prefatory statement in *Interim Report* [of the European Relief Council].

See entry no. 494.

111 Foreword to *Report on the National Collection by the Control Committee to the European Relief Council.* New York, 1921.

112 Foreword to *Waste In Industry,* by the Committee on Elimination of Waste in Industry of the Federated American Engineering Societies. Washington, D.C.: Federated Engineering Societies, 1921.

Later edition: New York: McGraw Hill Book Company, 1921.

113 Prefatory statement in *Final Report* [of the European Relief Council].

See entry no. 496.

114 Foreword to *The Balance of International Payments of the United States in 1922,* issued by the United States Bureau of Foreign and Domestic Commerce. *Trade Information Bulletin,* no. 144. Washington, D.C.: Government Printing Office, 1923.

115 Foreword to *Business Cycles and Unemployment: Report and Recommendations of a Committee of the President's Conference on Unemployment,* issued by the United States Department of Commerce. Elimination of Waste Series. Washington, D.C.: Government Printing Office, 1923.

Later edition: New York: McGraw-Hill Book Company, 1923.

116   Foreword to *How To Own Your Own Home: Handbook for Prospective Homeowners*, prepared by J. M. Gries and J. S. Taylor, and issued by the United States Bureau of Standards. Washington, D.C.: Government Printing Office, 1923.

117   Foreword to *Program of Activities of the Inter-American High Commission.*

   See entry no. 499.

118   Introduction to *Recommended Minimum Requirements for Small Dwelling Construction*, issued by the United States Bureau of Standards. Washington, D.C.: Government Printing Office, 1923.

119   Introduction to *The Stabilization of Business*, edited by Lionel D. Edie. New York: Macmillan Company, 1923.

120   Introduction to *Trade Association Activities*, prepared by L. E. Warford and R. A. May, and issued by the United States Bureau of Foreign and Domestic Commerce. Elimination of Waste Series, no. 319. Washington, D.C.: Government Printing Office, 1923.

121   Foreword to *The Balance of International Payments of the United States in 1923*, prepared by Rufus S. Tucker, and issued by the United States Bureau of Foreign and Domestic Commerce. *Trade Information Bulletin*, no. 215. Washington, D.C.: Government Printing Office, 1924.

   Also published as "Balance of International Payments." *Commerce Reports*, April 14, 1924, p. 75.

122   Foreword to *Better Homes in America Guidebook for Better Homes Campaign*. Better Homes in America publication no. 8. Washington, D.C.: Better Homes in America, 1924.

123   Foreword to *Commerce Yearbook, 1923*, issued by the United States Department of Commerce. Washington, D.C.: Government Printing Office, 1924.

124 Introduction to *The Place of Standardization in Modern Life.* by Albert W. Whitney. Washington, D.C.: Central Executive Council, Inter-American High Commission, 1924.

125 Foreword to *Seasonal Operation in Construction Industries: Summary of Report and Recommendations of a Committee of the President's Conference on Unemployment,* issued by the United States Department of Commerce. Elimination of Waste Series. Washington, D.C.: Government Printing Office, 1924.

126 Foreword to *Simplified Practice: What It Is and What It Offers,* issued by the United States Bureau of Standards. Washington, D.C.: Government Printing Office, 1924.

Also published as "Herbert Hoover Wars on Waste as Factor in People's Advance." *Public Service,* March 1925, p. 88.

127 Preface to *Transportation of Pacific Coast Perishables,* prepared by A. Lane Crichner, and issued by the United States Bureau of Foreign and Domestic Commerce. Trade Promotion Series, no. 12. Washington D.C.: Government Printing Office, 1924.

128 Foreword to *The Balance of International Payments of the United States in 1924,* prepared by Rufus S. Tucker, and issued by the United States Bureau of Foreign and Domestic Commerce. Trade Promotion Series, no. 340. Washington, D.C.: Government Printing Office, 1925.

Also published as "Balance of International Payments of the United States." *Commerce Reports,* May 18, 1925, pp. 379–380.

129 Foreword to *Better Homes in America Guidebook.* Better Homes in America publication no. 10. Washington, D.C.: Better Homes in America, 1925.

130 Foreword to *Commerce Yearbook, 1924,* issued by the United States Department of Commerce. Washington, D.C.: Government Printing Office, 1925.

131   Preface to *Everyman's House,* by Caroline Bartlett Crane. Garden City, New York: Doubleday, Page and Company, 1925.

132   Foreword to *National Directory of Commodity Specifications,* issued by the United States Bureau of Standards. Miscellaneous publication no. 65. Washington, D.C.: Government Printing Office, 1925.

133   Foreword to *The Plantation Rubber Industry in the Middle East,* prepared by David M. Figart, and issued by the United States Bureau of Foreign and Domestic Commerce. Trade Promotion Series, no. 2. Washington, D.C.: Government Printing Office, 1925.

Also published as "Crude-rubber Situation." *Commerce Reports.* June 8, 1925, p. 571.

134   Foreword to *The Stabilization of the Price of Wheat During the War and Its Effect Upon the Returns to the Producer,* by Frank M. Surface. Washington, D.C.: United States Grain Corporation, 1925.

135   Foreword to *Statistical Review of Review Operations* . . . [of the Commission for Relief in Belgium], by G. I. Gay.

See entry no. 504.

136   Foreword to *The Balance of International Payments of the United States in 1925,* prepared by Franklin W. Ryan, and issued by the United States Bureau of Foreign and Domestic Commerce. *Trade Information Bulletin,* no. 399. Washington, D.C.: Government Printing Office, 1926.

Also published as "America's Invisible Balance of Trade." In the *World Almanac and Book of Facts for 1927.* New York: New York World, 1927, pp. 186–187.

137   Foreword to *Better Homes in America Guidebook for Better Homes Campaigns.* Better Homes in America publication no. 12. Washington, D.C.: Better Homes in America, 1926.

138 Foreword to *Civil Aviation,* by the Joint Committee on Civil Aviation of the United States Department of Commerce and the American Engineering Council. Washington, D.C., 1926.

139 Foreword to *Congress of American Industry: Discussions by Leading Authorities, 1776–1926, as Presented at the Congress of American Industry, Philadelphia, September 7–27, 1926.* Philadelphia: Congress of American Industry, 1926.

140 Preface to *Emile Berlinger: Maker of the Microphone,* by Frederic Wile. Indianapolis, Indiana: Bobbs-Merrill Company, 1926.

141 Foreword to *Marketing of Short-Length Lumber: First Report of the Construction Sub-committee of the National Committee on Wood Utilization,* issued by the United States Department of Commerce. Washington, D.C.: Government Printing Office, 1926.

142 Foreword to *A New Departure in Higher Education: Facts and Comments about the New Policy by the Johns Hopkins University.* Baltimore, Maryland: Johns Hopkins University, 1926.

143 Foreword to *A Standard State Zoning Enabling Act Under Which Municipalities May Adopt Zoning Regulations,* by the Advisory Committee on Zoning of the United States Department of Commerce. Washington, D.C.: Government Printing Office, 1926.

Revised edition.

144 Foreword to *The Balance of International Payments of the United States in 1926,* prepared by Ray Hall, and issued by the United States Bureau of Foreign and Domestic Commerce. *Trade Information Bulletin,* no. 503. Washington, D.C.: Government Printing Office, 1927.

145 Introduction to *Five Years of the American Child Health Asso-*

ciation—A Bird's Eye View. New York: American Child Health Association, 1927.

146   Foreword to *May Day—Child Health Day 1927.* New York: American Child Health Association, 1927.

147   Foreword to *Packing for Domestic Shipment: Recommendations of the Advisory Board of the United States Department of Commerce on Domestic Packing,* issued by the United States Bureau of Foreign and Domestic Commerce. Domestic Commerce Series, nos. 10–16. Washington, D.C.: Government Printing Office, 1927.

148   Foreword to *Trade Association Activities,* prepared by Irving S. Paull, J. W. Millard, and James S. Taylor, and issued by the United States Bureau of Foreign and Domestic Commerce. Domestic Commerce Series, no. 20. Washington, D.C.: Government Printing Office, 1927.

149   Foreword to *Yearbook on Commercial Arbitration in the United States, 1927,* prepared under direction of the American Arbitration Association. New York: Oxford University Press, 1927.

150   Foreword to *The Balance of International Payments of the United States in 1927*, prepared by Ray Hall, and issued by the United States Bureau of Foreign and Domestic Commerce. *Trade Information Bulletin,* no. 552. Washington, D.C.: Government Printing Office, 1928.

151   Foreword entitled "The Forces of Our Economic Progress," to *A Century of Industrial Progress,* edited by Frederic W. Wile. Garden City, New York: published for the American Institute of the City of New York by Doubleday, Doran and Company, 1928.

152   Foreword to *City Planning Primer,* by the Advisory Committee on Zoning of the United States Department of Commerce. Washington, D.C.: Government Printing Office, 1928.

153 Foreword to *Present Home Financing Methods,* prepared by J. M. Gries and T. M. Curran, and issued by the United States Bureau of Standards. Washington, D.C.: Government Printing Office, 1928.

154 Foreword to *Standard City Planning Enabling Act,* by the Advisory Committee on City Planning and Zoning of the United States Department of Commerce. Washington, D.C.: Government Printing Office, 1928.

155 Foreword to *Frontiers of Trade,* by Julius Klein. New York: Century Company, 1929.

Also published in "Man Behind Our Exports," by Frederic W. Wile. *New York Herald Tribune Magazine,* June 9, 1929, p. 6.

156 "Dedication" [to David Starr Jordan], in *The Stanford Quad,* June 1930. Stanford, California: Associated Students of Stanford University, June 1930.

157 Prefatory message in *The Children's Charter,* by the White House Conference on Child Health and Protection, Washington, D.C., 1930. Washington, D.C., 1931.

158 Foreword to *The Writings of George Washington from the Original Manuscript Sources, 1745–1799,* edited by John Clement Fitzpatrick, prepared under the direction of the United States George Washington Bicentennial Committee, and published by the Authority of Congress. Volume 1. Washington, D.C.: Government Printing Office, 1931.

159 Foreword to *Final Reports of the President's Conference on Home Building and Home Ownership.* Washington, D.C., 1931. Volume 1. *Planning for Residential Districts,* edited by John M. Gries and James Ford. Washington, D.C., 1932.

160 Foreword to *Recent Social Trends in the United States,* by the President's Research Committee on Social Trends. New York: McGraw-Hill Book Company, 1933.

161   Prefatory message in *Mills College Yearbook, 1935.* Oakland, California, 1935.

162   Foreword to *Prospectus,* issued by the Industrial Hygiene Institute, Stanford University School of Medicine, San Francisco, California. Stanford, California: Stanford University Press, 1937.

163   Foreword to *Annual Booklet of the Pasadena Boys' Club.* Pasadena, California: Pasadena Foundation, 1938.

164   Foreword to *Money Raising, How To Do It,* by Irene Hazard Gerlinger. Los Angeles, California: Suttonhouse, 1938.

165   Foreword to *Journal As Ambassador to Great Britain,* by Charles Gates Dawes. New York: Macmillan Company, 1939.

166   Introduction to *The Belgian Campaign and the Surrender of the Belgian Army, May 10–28, 1940.* New York: Belgian American Educational Foundation, 1940.

167   Foreword to *Report to American Donors* . . . [of the Finnish Relief Fund].

See entry no. 518.

168   Foreword to *Special Collections in the Hoover Library on War, Revolution and Peace,* by Nina Almond and H. H. Fisher. Stanford, California: Stanford University Press, 1940.

Also published as "The Hoover Library on War, Revolution and Peace." In *Further Addresses Upon the American Road, 1938–1940* (entry no. 28), pp. 214–218.

169   Foreword to *Development of Mineral Industry Education in The United States,* by Thomas T. Read. Sponsored by Seeley W. Mudd Memorial Fund. New York: American Institute of Mining and Metallurgical Engineers, 1941.

First edition.

170 Introduction to *History of the United States Food Administration, 1917–1919*, by William Clinton Mullendore. Stanford, California: Stanford University Press, 1941.

171 Foreword to *Destruction at Our Expense: How Dismantling Factories in Germany Helps Inflation in the United States and Sabotages the Marshall Plan*, by Christopher Emmet and Fritz Baade. New York: Common Cause, 1947.

Also published as "Destruction at Our Expense." In *Addresses Upon the American Road, 1945–1948* (entry no. 32), p. 119.

172 Foreword to *No Reconstruction Without Food*. New York: Common Cause, 1948.

Also published as "On Feeding Germany." In *Addresses Upon the American Road, 1948–1950* (entry no. 33), pp. 167–168.

173 Foreword to *Low Income Families in the United States*, by Edward A. Keller. New York: American Economic Foundation, 1950.

174 Foreword to *The Power in the People,* by Felix Morley. New York: D. Van Nostrand Company, 1951.

Third edition.

175 Foreword to *Flight,* issued by the National Committee to Observe the 50th Anniversary of Powered Flight. Washington, D.C., 1953.

Also published as "On the Fiftieth Anniversary of Powered Flight." In *Addresses Upon the American Road, 1950–1955* (entry no. 38), pp. 332–333.

176 Foreword to *Fight for a City: The Story of the Union League Club of Chicago and Its Times, 1880–1955*, by Bruce Grant. Chicago: Rand McNally and Company, 1955.

177 Foreword to *The Hoover Report, 1953–1955: What It Means to*

You As a Citizen and Taxpayer, by Neil MacNeil and Harold W. Metz. New York: Macmillan Company, 1956.

Also published as "Foreword to the Hoover Report, 1953–1955." In *Addresses Upon the American Road, 1955–1960* (entry no. 40), pp. 256–257.

178 Introduction to *Hugh Gibson, 1883–1954: Extracts from His Letters and Anecdotes from His Friends,* edited by Perrin C. Galpin. New York: Belgian American Educational Foundation, 1956.

179 Foreword to *Our Nation's Water Resources, Policies and Politics: Lectures Given at the University of Chicago, April and May, 1956,* by Ben Moreell. Chicago: Law School, University of Chicago, 1956.

Also published as "On Water Resources and Government." In *Addresses Upon the American Road, 1955–1960* (entry no. 40), pp. 248–250.

180 Foreword to *The Role of Government in Developing Peaceful Uses of Atomic Energy,* by Arthur Kemp. National Economic Problem Series, no. 461. Washington, D.C.: American Enterprise Association, 1956.

Also published as "Peaceful Uses of Atomic Energy." In *Addresses Upon the American Road, 1955–1960* (entry no. 40), pp. 278–279.

181 Introduction to *Theodore E. Burton, American Statesman,* by Forrest Crissey. Cleveland, Ohio. World Publishing Company, 1956.

182 Foreword to *Always With Honour,* by Petr N. Vrangel. New York: Speller and Sons, 1957.

183 Foreword to *Society of Western Artists, 18th Annual Exhibition of Arts, November 6–December 8, 1957,* De Young Memorial Museum, San Francisco. N.p., 1957.

184 Foreword to *Economics of the Mineral Industries: A series of Articles by Specialists,* edited by Edward H. Robie. Seeley Mudd Series. New York: American Institute of Mining, Metallurgical and Petroleum Engineers, 1959.

Second edition.

Also published as "On Mining." In *Addresses Upon the American Road, 1955–1960* (entry no. 40), pp. 293–295.

185 Foreword to *The Memoirs of Ray Lyman Wilbur, 1875–1949,* edited by Edgar Eugene Robinson and Paul Carroll Edwards. Stanford, California: Stanford University Press, 1960.

186 Foreword to *Black Gold, the Story of An Oil Pioneer,* by Arthur Beeby-Thompson. Garden City, New York: Doubleday and Company, 1961.

First American edition.

187 Foreword to *100 Years and Millions of Boys: The Dynamic Story of the Boys' Clubs of America,* by William Edwin Hall. New York: Farrar, Straus and Cudahy, 1961.

Contributions to Periodicals and the Press

Articles

188 "And Their Deeds Are Remembered After Them." *Stanford Sequoia* 5 (1895–1896):225.

Also published with same title in Stanford Sequoia 21 (1912): 181–182.

189 "Some Notes on Crossings." *Mining and Scientific Press* 72 (February 1896):166–167.

Also published with same title in Mining and Scientific Press 120 (May 1920):743–744.

190 "Geology of the Four-Mile Placer Mining District, Colorado." *Engineering and Mining Journal* 63 (May 1897):510.

191 "The Superficial Alteration of Western Australian Ore-Deposits." *Transactions of the American Institute of Mining Engineers* 28 (October 1898):758–765.

192 "Mining and Milling Gold Ores in Western Australia." *Engineering and Mining Journal* 66 (December 1898):725–726.

193 "Training of Engineers." *Stanford Sequoia* 9 (October 1899): 54–55.

194 "Metal Mining in the Provinces of Chi-Li and Shantung, China." *Transactions of the Institution of Mining and Metallurgy* 8 (March 1900):324–331.

195 "Present Situation of the Mining Industry in China." *Engineering and Mining Journal* 69 (May 1900):619–620.

196 "The Kaiping Coal Mines and Coal Fields, Chihle Province, North China." *Transactions of the Institution of Mining and Metallurgy* 10 (June 1902):419–427.

Also published in part with same title in Engineering and Mining Journal 74 (August 1902):149–150.

197 "Gold Mining in Western Australia in 1902." *Engineering and Mining Journal* 75 (January 1903):18.

198 "Metallurgical Methods at Kalgoorlie, W.A." *Engineering and Mining Journal* 75 (March 1903):437.

199 "Gold Mine Accounts." *Engineering and Mining Journal* 76 (July 1903):44.

Also published with same title in The Economics of Mining (entry no. 80), pp. 31–33.

200 "Ore Treatment at Kalgoorlie." *Engineering and Mining Journal* 76 (August 1903):228.

Also published with same title in The Economics of Mining (entry no. 80), pp. 39–43.

201 Pritchard, W. A., co-author. "The Treatment of Sulpho-Telluride Ores at Kalgoorlie." *Engineering and Mining Journal* 76 (August 1903):156–157.

202 "The Future Gold Production in Western Australia." *Transactions of the Institution of Mining and Metallurgy* 13 (October 1903):1–13.

Also published in part as "Permanence in Depth in Kalgoorlie." *Engineering and Mining Journal* 76 (October 1903):655.

203 "The Economic Ratio of Treatment Capacity to Ore-Reserves." *Engineering and Mining Journal* 77 (March 1904):475–476.

Also published with same title in The Economics of Mining (entry no. 80), pp. 150–155.

204   "The Valuation of Gold Mines." *Engineering and Mining Journal* 77 (May 1904):801.

Also published with same title in The Economics of Mining (entry no. 80), pp. 185–189.

205   "Mine Valuation." *Engineering and Mining Journal* 78 (July 1904):5.

206   "Ore-Reserves and Treatment Capacity." *Engineering and Mining Journal* 78 (August 1904):253.

Also published as "Ore Reserves." In *The Economics of Mining* (entry no. 80), pp. 223–226.

207   "The Training of the Mining Engineer." *Science* 20 (November 1904):716–719.

Also published as "The Training for a Mining Engineer." *Stanford Alumnus* 6 (December 1904):4–8.

208   "Western Australia." *Engineering and Mining Journal* 79 (January 1905):41–42.

209   "Western Australian Gold Mining in 1905." *Engineering and Mining Journal* 81 (January 1906):136.

210   "Economics of a Boom." *The Mining Magazine* 6 (May 1912): 370–373.

211   "Is Gold Output Near Maximum?" *Annalist (New York Times),* April 21, 1913.

212   "Mining Engineers—Ancient and Mediaeval." *Mining Science* 70 (August 1914):25–27.

213   "Bind the Wounds of France." *National Geographic* 31 (May 1917):439–444.

214   "The Women's Call: Food Administrator Hoover Summons the

Women of America to the Colors." *Independent* 90 (June 23, 1917):568.

Also published as "Food Administration Invites Every Woman to Register and Sign Pledge." *United States Food Administration Bulletins*, nos. 1 and 2, (1917).

215 "Pooling the World Food Supply." *Country Gentleman* 82 (July 14, 1917):1133.

216 "What I Would Like Women to Do." *Ladies Home Journal,* August 1917, p. 25.

217 "A Letter to You From Mr. Hoover." *Good Housekeeping,* October 1917, p. 78.

218 "Why I Ask Your Help." *Ladies Home Journal,* October 1917, p. 18.

219 "National Policy for Grain and Livestock." *Black and White Record,* November 15, 1917, pp. 967–968+.

Also published as "Thoughts Concerning a National Policy for Grain and Livestock in Time of War." *United States Food Administration Bulletin,* no. 10 (1917).

220 "The New Food Card." *Journal of Home Economics* 10 (January 1918):21–22.

Also published as "Press Release no. 532." *United States Food Administration Press Releases,* volume 6 (1918).

221 "Food for All—A Fundamental War Problem." *Scientific American* 118 (April 6, 1918):310–311.

222 "Organize for Efficient Marketing." *Potato Magazine,* June 1918, p. 5.

223 "Outline by Herbert Hoover ... How Boys and Girls Can

Assist the Food Administration." *Sierra Educational News* 14 (June 1918):334.

224   "Personal Message from Food Administrator to the Teachers of the Public Schools of California." *Sierra Educational News* 14 (June 1918):324.

225   "Renewal of the Appeal for Belgian Relief Organizations." *C.R.B. Bulletin*, no. 5 (July 8, 1918):8.

226   "Food for Our Allies in 1919." *National Geographic* 34 (September 1918):242–244.

Also published as "Press Release no. 1206." *United States Food Administration Press Releases*, volume 13 (1918).

227   "How America Has Fed the Allies." *Current History* 8, part 2 (September 1918):450–451.

228   "The Food Future: What Every American Mouthful Means to Europe." *Forum* 61 (February 1919):210–218.

229   "Why We Are Feeding Germany." *A.R.A. Bulletin*, no. 3 (April 1, 1919):2–3.

Published by American Relief Administration.

230   "Food Prospects for the Coming Harvest Year." *A.R.R. Bulletin*. no. 12 (June 16, 1919):1–3.

Published by American Relief Administration.

231   "The Economic Situation in Europe." *A.R.A. Bulletin*, no. 18 (July 18, 1919):1–6.

Published by American Relief Administration.

Also published with same title in World's Work 39 (November 1919):98–101; "Memorandum on the Economic Situation." *American Academy of Political and Social Sciences Annals* 87 (January 1920):106–111.

232 "Some Notes on Industrial Readjustment." *Saturday Evening Post*, December 27, 1919, pp. 3–4+.

Also published as "National Welfare Defined Industrially." In *Vital Forces in Current Events*, edited by Morris E. Speare and Walter B. Norris. New York: Ginn and Company, 1920, pp. 93–95.

233 "Herbert Hoover on Europe's Coal Situation." *Street*, December 1919, pp. 3–4+.

234 "Marketing American Surplus Food Products." *Farm and Home*, January 1920, p. 5+.

235 "Ills We Inherit from the War." *Woman's Home Companion*, March 1920, p. 4.

236 "Some Notes on Agricultural Readjustment and High Cost of Living." *Saturday Evening Post*, April 10, 1920, pp. 3–4+.

Also published as "Herbert Hoover on High Cost of Living." *Business Digest and Investment Weekly*, May 25, 1920, pp. 663–665+.

237 "Economic, Social and Industrial Problems Confronting the Nation: Maintenance of Our National Ideals." *Trust Companies*, April 1920, pp. 349–352.

238 "The Next Generation." *Quaker*, May 28, 1920, pp. 27–28.

239 "America and You." *Open Road*, May 1920, pp. 5–8+.

240 "How America Helped Starving Europe." *World Outlook*, June 1920, pp. 4–5.

241 "Neighborhood Houses Help Solve Social Problems." *Better Times*, June 1920, p. 16.

242 "The Battle Line of Hunger." *McClure's*, July 1920, pp. 27–28+.

243 "Herbert Hoover Says Waterway Necessary." *Detroiter*, July 1920, p. 10.

244 "Thrift and American Women." *Ladies Home Journal*, August 1920, p. 3+.

245 "Child Life in Central Europe and the Need of Cooperation in Relief." *A.R.A. Bulletin*, no. 1, second series (October 1, 1920): 1–3.

Published by American Relief Administration.

Also published as "Child Life in Central Europe." *World's Work* 41 (December 1920):130–131.

246 "A Letter from Mr. Hoover." *Literary Digest*, October 30, 1920, p. 22.

Also published with same title in Mining and Metallurgy, December 1920, p. 34.

247 "America's Care of Millions of European Children Since the Armistice: First Year to August 1919." *A.R.A. Bulletin*, no. 4, second series (November 15, 1920):2–8.

Published by American Relief Administration.

Also published as "Three Million Starving Children Crying to America." *Current Opinion* 69 (November 1920):611–616.

248 "An Announcement." *Saturday Evening Post*, November 20, 1920, p. 25+.

Also published as Three and One Half Million Children to Save: An Announcement. European Relief Council, 1920. (Pamphlet.) "$33,000,000 to Feed Europe's Children." *Stanford Illustrated Review*, January 1921, p. 144+.

249 "Collier's Strike Cure—and Its Critics." *Collier's*, November 27, 1920, pp. 9–10+.

250 "The Opportunity of the Engineering Profession." *Mining and Metallurgy*, November 1920, p. 4.

251 "The Appeal of Hungry Children to the American Community

Chest." *A.R.A. Bulletin,* no. 5, second series (December 1, 1920):1–5.

Published by American Relief Administration.

252 "Peace on Earth, Good Will to Men: A Christmas Message to the American People." *Independent* 104 (December 25, 1920): 419–420.

253 "How Much Longer Must We Feed Europe?" *A.R.A. Bulletin,* no. 7, second series (December 31, 1920):2–4.

Published by American Relief Administration.

Also published with same title in Forum 64 (December 1920): 377–379.

254 "The Housing Problem: A Direct Message for Responsible Industrial Executives." *Industrial Management* 60 (December 1920):424a–424b.

255 "America's Magnificent Opportunity." *Weekly Review* 4 (January 5, 1921):9.

256 "The Children Must Be Saved." *A.R.A. Bulletin,* no. 9, second series (February 1, 1921):2.

Published by American Relief Administration.

257 "The Friendship of Food." *Metropolitan,* February 1921, p. 20+.

258 "To Break the Vicious Circle." *Nation's Business,* February 1921, p. 17.

259 "What Peace Has Done to Europe." Review of *It Might Have Happened to You,* by Coningsby Dawson. *New York Times Book Review,* March 27, 1921, p. 1+.

260 "Relief for Europe." *International Conciliation,* no. 160 (March 1921):111–112.

261 "What America Faces." *Industrial Management* 61 (April 1, 1921):225–229.

262 "Fact Information in Business: A Message to Special Librarians." *Special Libraries* 12 (April 1921):61.

Also published with same title in Commercial Libraries and the Department of Commerce, edited by Dorsey W. Hyde, Jr. Washington, D.C.: Special Libraries Association, 1922, pp. 20–21. (Pamphlet.)

263 "Facing Our Economic Facts." *Columbia* (Knights of Columbus), August 1921, p. 3.

264 "Cooperation of the Department of Commerce with the Mineral Industry." *Mining Congress Journal* 7 (November 1921):470.

265 "International Confidence Renewed by Arms Conference." *Current Affairs*, December 26, 1921, p. 4.

266 "Educational Evolution." *Stanford Quad*, 1921, p. 52.

267 "Your Automotive Industry." *Collier's*, January 7, 1922, p. 5.

268 "A Way Out of the Railroad Tangle." *Nation's Business*, March 1922, p. 12.

269 "American Individualism: The Genius of Our Government and Our Industry Reaffirmed Against Old World Philosophies." *World's Work* 43 (April 1922):584–588.

270 "Adjusting the Department of Commerce to Our Export Needs." *Export Trade*, May 6, 1922, pp. 7–8.

271 "The Present Condition of Our Foreign Trade." *Commerce Reports*, May 8, 1922, p. 223.

272 "The Broadcasts of Tomorrow." *Popular Science Monthly*, July 1922, p. 19.

273 "Radio's Great Future." *Radio Broadcast* 1 (September 1922): 433.

274 "The Home as an Investment." *Delineator*, October 1922, p. 17+.

275 "Policing the Ether." *Scientific American* 127 (August 1922): 80.

276 "The Urgent Need for Radio Legislation." *Radio Broadcast* 2 (January 1923):211.

277 "Washington the Engineer." *American Legion Weekly*, February 16, 1923, p. 8.

278 "A Bill of Rights." *Mother and Child* 4 (February 1923):81.

Also published as "A Child's Bill of Rights." *New York Herald Tribune Magazine*, May 1, 1927, p. 1+; "A Child's Bill of Rights." *Child Welfare* 24 (November 1929):122.

279 "Why We Pay Thirty Per Cent Too Much for Our Coal." *Industrial Management* 65 (February 1923):65–66.

280 "Ideals in American Education." *Journal of National Education Association*, March 1923, p. 79.

Also published as "To Give All a Fair Start." *Trained Men*, June 1923, p. 138.

281 "A Personal Message to the Executives Who Read *Industrial Management*." *Industrial Management* 65 (March):130.

282 "Pro-Work and Anti-War." *Woman Citizen*, April 21, 1923, p. 7.

283 "Jew As Philanthropist." *Jewish Tribune*, September 7, 1923, p. 9.

284 "Alaska Salmon Protection." *Outdoor America*, December 1923, pp. 196–198.

285 "A Distinct Step in Progress." *Nation's Business*, December 1923, p. 41.

286 "Economic Prospects of 1924." *Commerce Reports*, January 7, 1924, pp. 15–16.

287 "Our Foreign Trade in Favorable Position." *Annalist (New York Times)*, January 7, 1924, p. 13.

288 "A Message to the Mining Industries." *Engineering and Mining Journal Press* 117 (January 19, 1924):81.

289 "Railroad Consolidation." *Saturday Evening Post*, February 9, 1924, pp. 6–7+.

290 "Superpower and Its Public Relations." *Military Engineer* 16 (July–August 1924):278–282.

291 "Wanted: A Lifting Purpose." *Open Road*, November 1924, pp. 25–27.

292 "The South's Great Progress in Foreign Trade." *Manufacturer's Record*, part 2 (*South's Development*), December 1, 1924, pp. 131–133.

293 "Herbert Hoover to Coal Exporters." *Black Diamond* 73 (December 27, 1924):723.

294 "Government and Power Development." *English Review* 39 (December 1924):786–796.

295 "Economic Prospects of the New Year." *Commerce Reports*, January 5, 1925, pp. 13–14.

296 "Export Trade Expected to Increase in 1925." *Annalist (New York Times)*, January 5, 1925, pp. 13–14.

297 "The Long View of Farming." *Country Gentleman*, January 10, 1925, p. 3.

298 "A Message from Herbert Hoover." *Modern Miller*, February 10, 1925, p. 65.

299 "Findings of Safety Conference Receive Nation-wide Consideration." *American City* 32 (March 1925):249–250.

300 "Secretary Hoover's Views." *Nation* 120 (April 29, 1925):492.

301 "What Men Should Know About Homes." *Delineator*, April 1925, p. 11.

302 "May Day Belongs to the Children." *Collier's*, May 2, 1925, p. 23.

303 "Fit—Or Unfit?" *Delineator*, May 1925, pp. 8–9.

304 "Home Training and Citizenship." *Child Welfare* 19 (May 1925):p. 479.

305 "May Day—Child Health Day—1925." *McClure's*, May 1925, pp. 35–38.

306 "More and Better Fishing." *Liberty*, June 20, 1925, p. 25.

307 "To Remember the Child Wisely Will Become a National Habit." *Child Welfare* 19 (July 1925):591.

308 "No Imposition of Government in Business." *Factory: The Magazine of Management*, October 1925, p. 536.

Title from table of contents.

309 "A Problem We Must Solve." *Farm and Fireside*, December 1925, p. 3+.

310 "Economic Prospects for 1926." *Commerce Reports*, January 4, 1926, pp. 9–10.

311 "The Questions Mr. Hoover Asks." *New York Times*, January 10, 1926, section 8, p. 1.

312 "Tire Users Can Solve Rubber Situation." *American Motorist*, February 1926, p. 8+.

313 "Waterways—the Farmer's Need." *Country Gentleman*, March 1926, pp. 3–4+.

314 "The Home and the Nation." *Child Welfare* 20 (April 1926): 450.

315 "Our Goal the Normal Child." *Forecast*, July 1926, p. 11+.

316 "Water Power and the Pork Barrel." *New York Herald Tribune*, September 26, 1926, pp. 4–5.

317 "Aviation from Federal Viewpoint." *California Journal of Development*, September 30, 1926, pp. 7–8+.

318 "The Search for the Perfect Child." *Forum* 76 (October 1926): 537–542.

319 "Economic Prospects for the Coming Year." *Commerce Reports*, January 3, 1927, pp. 12–13.

320 "Hoover Predicts Auto Demand Will Become Greater." *New York Evening Post Annual Automobile Number*, January 8, 1927, section 6, p. 1.

321 "Home Building and Home Ownership: Their National Significance." *Child Welfare* 21 (April 1927):357–358.

322 "Opening the St. Lawrence." *Farm Journal*, April 1927, p. 13+.

323 "National Program for Street and Highway Safety." *California Journal of Development*, May 2, 1927, p. 5+.

324 "Equipment Since the Centennial." *American Machinist* 66 (May 19, 1927):821.

325 "America's Greatest Asset." *Children,* May 1927, p. 7.

326 "The Problem of the Mississippi Flood." *Editor and Publisher,* July 2, 1927, p. 11.

327 "Columbia—Gem of Airways." *New York Herald Tribune Magazine,* August 7, 1927, pp. 1–2.

Also published as "Aviation and the Department of Commerce." *Transportation Magazine,* April 1928, pp. 48–49; "Civil Aviation's Rapid Progress." *Aero Digest,* April 1928, p. 509+.

328 "A Statement from Secretary Hoover to Readers of the *American City.*" *American City* 37 (November 1927):575–576.

329 "The Importance of Education for Home Life." *Child Welfare* 22 (April 1928):347.

330 "A Message to the *Tariff Review* from Herbert Hoover." *Tariff Review* 79 (July 1928):223.

331 "A Message of World Wide Influence." *Manufacturer's Record,* November 15, 1928, pp. 62–63.

332 "Better Homes." *Child Welfare* 23 (April 1929):402.

333 "Message to Teachers." *Sierra Educational News,* February 1930, p. 15.

334 "From President Hoover to *Ladies Home Journal.*" *Ladies Home Journal,* June 1932, p. 5.

335 "The Scientific Work of the Government of the United States." *Scientific Monthly* 36 (January 1933):7+.

336 "I am a Fisherman." *Stanford Chaparral,* March 1936, p. 24.

337   "The Crisis and the Political Parties." *Atlantic Monthly* 160 (September 1937):257–268.

Also published as "The Crisis and the Political Parties and an American Program." In *Addresses Upon the American Road, 1933–1938* (entry no. 24), pp. 243–263.

338   "Principles of American System of Liberty Laid Down in 'Bill of Rights'." *Pro America* (San Francisco), September 1937, pp. 1–2.

339   "President Roosevelt's Foreign Policy." *Liberty*, April 15, 1939, pp. 5–8.

Also published as "Foreign Policies Today." In *Further Addresses Upon the American Road, 1938–1940* (entry no. 28), pp. 104–115; "President Roosevelt's Foreign Policy." In *Shall We Send Our Boys to Foreign Wars?* (entry no. 27), pp. 1–3.

340   "Three Million Boys Challenge America." *This Week*, July 2, 1939, p. 6+.

341   "We Must Keep Out." *Saturday Evening Post*, October 28, 1939, pp. 8–9.

Also published with same title in Further Addresses Upon the American Road, 1938–1940 (entry no. 28), pp. 139–157.

342   "Russian Misadventure." *Collier's*, April 27, 1940, pp. 21–22+.

Also published with same title in Further Addresses Upon the American Road, 1938–1940 (entry no. 28), pp. 158–171.

343   "Two Great Reasons Why We Must Keep Out of the War." *Liberty*, June 15, 1940, pp. 8–10.

Also published as "The Nine Horsemen and America." In *Further Addresses Upon the American Road, 1938–1940* (entry no. 28), pp. 172–182.

344 "It Needn't Happen Here." *American Mercury,* July 1940, pp. 263–270.

Also published with same title in Addresses Upon the American Road, 1940–1941 (entry no. 29), pp. 165–173.

Published in part, with same title, in Reader's Digest, September 1940, pp. 73–76.

345 "Food and War." *Christian Science Monitor Magazine,* November 23, 1940, pp. 1–2.

346 "Feed Hungry Europe." *Collier's,* November 23, 1940, p. 12+.

Also published as When Winter Comes to Europe, N.p., n.d. (Pamphlet.)

347 "Friend of Belgians States King's Case." *Life,* November 25, 1940, p. 75.

348 "Hope in a Poorer World." *Rotarian,* February 1941, pp. 8–11.

349 "Protect Democracy: Vote, Says Ex-president Herbert Hoover." *Pathfinder,* October 24, 1942, p. 3.

350 "We'll Have to Feed the World Again." *Collier's,* November 28, 1942, pp. 11–12+, December 5, 1942, p. 17+.

351 "Organization for Food Supply." *Farm Journal and Farmer's Wife,* December 1942, p. 18.

Also published with same title, in Addresses Upon the American Road, 1941–1945 (entry no. 31), pp. 265–268.

352 "Home Front Vital Hoover Declares." *New York Times,* January 12, 1943, p. 7.

Also published as "Article 1." In Addresses Upon the American Road, 1941–1945 (entry no. 31), pp. 179–181; *The Home Fronts and Global Strategy* (entry no. 77), pp. 3–5.

353   "Strain in Germany Studied by Hoover." *New York Times*, January 13, 1943, p. 10.

Also published as "Article 2." In *Addresses Upon the American Road, 1941–1945* (entry no. 31), pp. 181–184; *The Home Fronts and Global Strategy* (entry no. 77), pp. 6–7.

354   "Japanese Supplies Good, Hoover Says." *New York Times*, January 14, 1943, p. 8.

Also published as "Article 3." In *Addresses Upon the American Road, 1941–1945* (entry no. 31), pp. 184–187; *The Home Fronts and Global Strategy* (entry no. 77), pp. 9–11.

355   "Home Front Tasks Defined by Hoover." *New York Times*, January 15, 1943, p. 2.

Also published as "Article 4." In *Addresses Upon the American Road, 1941–1945* (entry no. 31), pp. 187–190; *The Home Fronts and Global Strategy* (entry no. 77), pp. 12–14.

356   "U.S. War Council Urged by Hoover." *New York Times*, January 16, 1943, p. 4.

Also published as "Article 5." In *Addresses Upon the American Road, 1941–1945* (entry no. 31), pp. 190–192; *The Home Fronts and Global Strategy* (entry no. 77), pp. 15–17.

357   "Hoover Envisages Attrition of Axis." *New York Times*, January 17, 1943, p. 12.

Also published as "Article 6." In *Addresses Upon the American Road, 1941–1945* (entry no. 31), pp. 192–195; *The Home Fronts and Global Strategy* (entry no. 77), pp. 18–20.

358   "Mr. Hoover's Reply." *What's New in Foods and Nutrition*, January 1943, pp. 4–5.

359   "In the Name of Humanity." *Christian Advocate*, February 11, 1943.

Also published with same title in Addresses Upon the American Road, 1941–1945 (entry no. 31), pp. 305–311.

360 Gibson, Hugh, co-author. "Feed the Starving Now." *Collier's*, February 20, 1943, p. 11+.

Also published with same title in Addresses Upon the American Road, 1941–1945 (entry no. 31), pp. 312–323.

Also published in part with same title in Reader's Digest, April 1943, pp. 16–18.

361 "In This Time of Dreadful Trial." *Young People's Weekly Magazine of Christian Living*, February 21, 1943, pp. 5–6.

362 Gibson, Hugh, co-author. "An Approach to Lasting Peace." *New York Times Magazine*, April 4, 1943, p. 5.

Also published with same title in Addresses Upon the American Road, 1941–1945 (entry no. 31), pp. 57–63.

Also published in part with same title in Reader's Digest, June 1943, pp. 10–12.

363 "The Fifth Freedom." *Rotarian*, April 1943, pp. 8–9.

Also published with same title in Addresses Upon the American Road, 1941–1945 (entry no. 31), pp. 222–225.

364 "Food Is Ammunition." *Woman*, July 1943, pp. 8–9.

365 "Enchanted World." *This Week*, August 1, 1943, p. 2.

Also published with same title in Addresses Upon the American Road, 1941–1945 (entry no. 31), pp. 393–394.

366 Gibson, Hugh, co-author. "History's Greatest Murder Trial." *This Week*, August 29, 1943, pp. 4–5.

Also published with same title in Addresses Upon the American Road, 1941–1945 (entry no. 31), pp. 64–70.

367 "The Futility of Military Alliances." *Collier's*, November 6, 1943, pp. 21–22+.

Also published with same title in Addresses Upon the American Road, 1941–1945 (entry no 31), pp. 97–107.

368 "A New Way to Make Peace." *This Week*, November 7, 1943, pp. 4–5.

369 "Has U.S.A. Designs on the Union?" *Forum* (South Africa) 6 (January 15, 1944):5.

370 "When the Boys Come Home." *Collier's*, February 5, 1944, p. 22+.

Also published as "A Preliminary Program of Reconstruction." In *Addresses Upon the American Road, 1941–1945* (entry no. 31), pp. 226–241.

371 Gibson, Hugh, co-author. "World Peace—Women Can Win It." *Woman's Home Companion*, February 1944, pp. 26–27+.

372 "Let's Go Fishin'." *Collier's*, April 22, 1944, pp. 18+.

Also published with same title in Addresses Upon the American Road, 1941–1945 (entry no. 31), pp. 400–406.

373 "The Front of Human Decency." *Woman's Home Companion*, April 1944, p. 26+.

Also published with same title in Addresses Upon the American Road, 1941–1945 (entry no. 31), pp. 395–399.

374 "The Case for Children." *Human Events*, May 17, 1944.

375 "Wider Oaks Plan Urged by Hoover." *New York Times*, March 25, 1945, p. 29.

Also published as "The Seven Points that Dumbarton Oaks Forgot." *Congressional Record*, 79th Congress, first session, 1945, 91, part 11:A1488; "Article 1." In *Addresses Upon the American Road, 1941–1945* (entry no. 31), pp. 111–113; *Some Additions to the Dumbarton Oaks Proposals* (entry no. 78), pp. 3–6.

376 "Hoover Asks That Political Rights be Proclaimed in Peace Charter." *New York Times*, March 26, 1945, p. 13.

Also published as "Article 2." In *Addresses Upon the American*

Road, 1941–1945 (entry no. 31), pp. 113–115; *Some Additions to the Dumbarton Oaks Proposals* (entry no. 78), pp. 6–8.

377 "Hoover Asks Pacts Be Open to Change." *New York Times,* March 27, 1945, p. 11.

Also published as "Article 3." In *Addresses Upon the American Road, 1941–1945* (entry no. 31), pp. 115–119; *Some Additions to the Dumbarton Oaks Proposals* (entry no. 78), pp. 8–13.

378 "Hoover Proposals for Disarmament." *New York Times,* March 28, 1945, p. 16.

Also published as "The Warning Came Early." *Nation* 179 (October 23, 1954): 353; "Article 4." In *Addresses Upon the American Road, 1941–1945* (entry no. 31), pp. 119–123; *Some Additions to the* Dumbarton Oaks Proposals (entry no. 78), pp. 13–17.

379 "Food for Liberated Countries." *Messenger,* July 10, 1945, pp. 10–12.

380 "The Right to Strike." *This Week,* December 29, 1946, p. 9.

Also published with same title in Addresses Upon the American Road, 1945–1948 (entry no. 32), pp. 55–57.

381 "Herbert Hoover's Plan for Palestine." *Plain Talk,* March 1948, pp. 32–33.

382 "They Look to Us." *This Week,* May 2, 1948, p. 2.

383 "The Miracle of America." *Woman's Home Companion,* November 1948, p. 33.

Also published with same title in Addresses Upon the American Road, 1948–1950 (entry no. 33), pp. 3–7.

384 "The Uncommon Man." *This Week,* February 6, 1949, p. 2.

Also published with same title in This Week, August 5, 1956, p. 2; *Addresses Upon the American Road, 1955–1960* (entry no. 40), p. 92.

385 "To Lighten Their Darkness." *Reader's Digest*, February 1949, verso of back cover.

Also published with same title in Addresses Upon the American Road, 1948–1950 (entry no. 33), p. 173.

386 "The Reform of Government." *Fortune*, May 1949, pp. 73–75.

Also published with same title in Addresses Upon the American Road, 1948–1950 (entry no. 33), pp. 146–152.

387 "The City Versus Boys." *Rotarian*, April 1950, pp. 7–8.

Also published with same title in Addresses Upon the American Road, 1950–1955 (entry no. 38), pp. 277–281.

388 "The Gifts of Nature." *Natural History*, April 1950, p. 146.

389 "The Citizen's Responsibility to America Today." *American Druggist*, July 1950, p. 70.

Also published as "On Representative Government." In *Addresses Upon the American Road, 1948–1950* (entry no. 33), pp. 50–51.

390 Morley, Felix, joint reviewer. "Great Quaker." Review of *Rufus Jones: Master Quaker*, by David Hinshaw. *Freeman* 1 (June 4, 1951):571–572.

Also published with same title in Addresses Upon the American Road 1950–1955 (entry no. 38), pp. 305–308.

391 "Men Are Equal Before Fish." *Florida Speaks*, November 1951, pp. 42+.

Also published with same title in Addresses Upon the American Road, 1950–1955 (entry no. 38), pp. 310–311.

392 "We Have Just Begun to Dream." *American Weekly*, May 25, 1952, pp. 4–5.

Also published with same title in Addresses Upon the American Road, 1950–1955 (entry no. 38), pp. 192–195.

393 "A Warning from Herbert Hoover." *This Week*, December 28, 1952, p. 7.

Also published as "What's Happened to the Two Party System." In *Addresses Upon the American Road, 1950–1955* (entry no. 38), pp. 138–139.

394 "Can We Ever Have Peace With Russia?" *This Week*, February 6, 1955, p. 7+.

Also published as "Can We Ever Have Peace with the Russians?" In *Addresses Upon the American Road, 1950–1955* (entry no. 38), pp. 101–103.

395 "Radio Gets a Policeman." *American Heritage*, August 1955, pp. 73–76.

Also published with same title in Addresses Upon the American Road, 1955–1960 (entry no. 40), pp. 267–275.

396 "Why Balance the Budget?" *This Week*, December 11, 1955, p. 7+.

Also published with same title in Addresses Upon the American Road, 1955–1960 (entry no. 40), pp. 218-220.

397 "The Leadership I Believe In." *This Week*, June 10, 1956, p. 2.

398 "How to Build a Better Tomorrow." *This Week*, May 26, 1957, p. 2.

Also published with same title in Addresses Upon the American Road, 1955–1960 (entry no. 40), p. 109.

399 "What Is a Boy?" *Ladies Home Journal*, October 1957, p. 220.

Also published with same title in Addresses Upon the American Road, 1955–1960 (entry no. 40), p. 341.

400 Nichols, Marie Therese, co-author. "Myth of the Fourth Horseman." *Saturday Review*, September 20, 1958, p. 17+.

Also published with same title in Addresses Upon the American Road, 1955–1960 (entry no. 40), pp. 383–387.

401 "Former President Hoover Says: We Need a U.S. Crime Census." *This Week*, June 7, 1959, pp. 8–9+.

Also published as "We Must Know More About Crime." In *Addresses Upon the American Road, 1955–1960* (entry no. 40), pp. 141–148.

Also published in part as "Do We Have A Duty to Get Tough?" *Reader's Digest*, September 1959, pp. 143–146.

402 "Thank You, Miss Gray." *Reader's Digest*, July 1959, pp. 118–120.

Also published with same title in Addresses Upon the American Road, 1955–1960 (entry no. 40), pp. 319–321.

403 "It's Tough to Be a Statue." *This Week*, February 18, 1962, pp. 10–13.

404 "From Herbert Hoover on His Ninetieth Birthday." *Reader's Digest*, September 1964, p. 143–144.

Contributions to Articles

405 Contribution to a discussion of early mining laws. *Published in* "Meetings of Sections." *Mining and Metallurgical of America Bulletin*, June 30, 1914, pp. 122–123.

406 "Mr. Hoover's Conclusions." In "German War Practices: Part 1: Treatment of Civilians." *United States Committee on Public Information*, January 1918, p. 79.

Also published as "Mr. Hoover's Scathing Testimony." In "German Ruthlessness." *Current History* 7, part 2 (February 1918):350.

407 "The College Student and the War." In "Universities and War," by Frank Diehl Fackenthal. *Stanford Illustrated Review* 19 (1918):214.

408 Statement on shipping.
Published in "What Three Prominent Presidential Candidates Have to Say About Shipping." *Nautical Gazette* 98 (June 5, 1920):843–844.

409 Statement on trade relations with Russia.
Published in "Trade Relations with Soviet Russia." *Commerce Reports*, March 26, 1921, p. 1713.

410 Statement on farm prosperity.
Published in "New Factors Insure Farm Prosperity." *Farm and Home*, September 1921, p. 5+.

411 "The Chamber of Commerce." In "Log of Organized Business." *Nation's Business*, December 1921, p. 46.

412 Statement on the textile industry and the Department of Commerce.
Published in "Your Industry and Our Government." *Textile World*, February 1922, p. 131.

413 "Secretary Hoover's Appreciation." In "A Convention of Constructive Ideas," by D. M. Edwards. *American Industries*, June 1922, p. 9.

414 "Holds Rise in Credits Is Necessary." In "What Is Happening in World of Business Today?" *Capper's Farmer*, June 1923, p. 34.

415 "Mr. Hoover Shows Interest." In "Chatting with Cabinet Secretaries," by Charles A. Lyman. *Spotlight*, July 1, 1923, pp. 17–18.

416 "Rapid Recovery from 'Most Violent Commodity Slump in Our

History'." In "How Cabinet Officials View National Situation."
Magazine of Wall Street 31 (December 23, 1923):298–299.

417   Statement on the American Child Health Association.
Published in "The Nervous Child and the Spoiled Child," by
James J. Walsh and John A. Foote. *Ladies Home Journal*,
December 1923, p. 36.

418   "A Prosperous Year Should Follow . . ." In "How Shall We Plan
for 1924?" *System* 45 (February 1924):161.

419   Statement on elimination of waste in the lumber industry.
Published in "Battle of the Thirty-second," by W. DuB. Brook-
ings. *Nation's Business*, February 1924, p. 20.

420   Tribute.
Published in "Doctor L. Emmett Holt." *Child Health Magazine*
5 (February 1924):42.

421   "Hoover Takes Stand on Question." In "Religion A La 'King
Telephone'." *Radio Digest Illustrated*, March 22, 1924, p. 2

422   "From Secretary Hoover, Department of Commerce." In
"Opinions from Cabinet Committee." *Playground* 18 (July
1924):198.

423   Statement on elimination of waste through simplification.
Published in "Simplification: Achievement and Promise," by
P. G. Agnew. *Factory: The Magazine of Management*, January
1925, p. 26.

424   "Hoover Optimistic." In "1925 in 100 One-Minute Interviews."
Forbes 15 (February 1, 1925):535.

425   "Herbert Hoover Issues Proclamation on 'Help Save the Children'." In "Child Health Day," by Alida S. Malkus. *Success*,
May 1925, p. 10.

426 "Herbert Hoover's Plea." In "Start May First." *Woman's Home Companion*, May 1925, p. 5.

427 Statement on the Department of Commerce and the Patent Office.
Published in "Herbert Hoover and the Patent Office." *Scientific American*, June 1925, p. 373.

428 "Advances Toward Economic Ideals." In "At the Turn of a Quarter Century." *Review of Reviews* 73 (January 1926):32.

429 Statement on foreign trade and the Department of Commerce.
Published in "Commercial Exploration," by Isaac F. Marcosson. *Saturday Evening Post*, February 13, 1926, pp. 53–54. (Article begins p. 8); *Caravans of Commerce*, by Isaac F. Marcosson. New York: Harper and Brothers Publishers, 1926, pp. 31–43.

430 Statement on development of waterways to save money.
Published in "Marching With Hoover to the Sea." *Liberty*, May 22, 1926, pp. 75–78.

431 "Face Powder or Pure Science?" In "Pure Science Pays Its Way," by Edwin E. Slosson. *Nation's Business*, June 1926, p. 26.

432 Statement on the causes of American prosperity.
Published in "The Basis of American Prosperity," by Isaac F. Marcosson. *Saturday Evening Post*, July 31, 1926, pp. 4–5. (Article begins p. 3.)

433 Statement on Independence Day.
Published in "In Celebration of Independence Day." *National Republic*, July 1926, p. 9.

434 "Secretary Hoover." In "Leaders in United States, Japan United in Praise of Sesqui-Centennial." *Japan Advertiser*, October 10, 1926 (Sesqui-Centennial International Exposition Special Edition), p. 3.

435 Statement on the need for spiritual leadership.
Published in "What the Big Wigs Say." *Farm Life*, December 1926, p. 18.

436 "Secretary Hoover's Views." In "Management Week Review of Waste Elimination." *American Accountant*, March 1927, p. 5.

437 "The Department of Commerce." In "Air Pioneering: The Government's Contribution to the Future of Commercial Aviation." *Magazine of Business* 54 (August 1928):138–139.

438 Statement on the value of insurance.
Published in "What the Candidates Have to Say About Insurance." *Life Aetna-izer*, October 1928, p. 11.

439 "The Three Purgatories." In "The Real Calvin Coolidge." *Good Housekeeping*, May 1935, p. 247.

440 Statement on most memorable childhood book.
Published in "My Most Memorable Childhood Book." *Better Homes and Gardens*, December 1957, p. 10.

441 Statement on the importance of the vice-presidency.
Published in "No One Should Turn Down the Vice-Presidency," by James P. Mitchell. *This Week*, May 1, 1960, p. 6.

*Selected Interviews** *

442 Irwin, Will. "First Aid to America." *Saturday Evening Post*, March 24, 1917, pp. 6–7+.

443 Wilhelm, Donald. "Waste Not, Want Not." *Independent* 90 (June 9, 1917):459–460.

* Interviews written primarily in Hoover's own words.

444 Wolff, William A. "Hoover Talks." *Collier's*, October 12, 1918, pp. 5–6+.

445 Barry, Richard. "We Ought to be Thankful." *Pictorial Review*, March 1920, p. 5+.

446 "Self-Expression Is Need of Today." *Business Methods*, November 1920, p. 11.

447 "A Statement by Herbert Hoover on World Food Problems." *American Food Journal*, March 1921, pp. 8–10.

448 Marcosson, Isaac F. "American Relief—And After." *Saturday Evening Post*, April 30, 1921, pp. 21–22+.

Also published as "Children's Relief and Democracy." *A.R.A. Bulletin*, no. 15, second series (August 1, 1921), p. 1. *Published by* American Relief Administration.

449 Forbes, B. C. "Hoover Tells How to Preserve American Living Standards." *Forbes*, April 29, 1922, pp. 65–66.

450 Knappen, Theodore M. "Making Profits by Cutting Waste." *Magazine of Wall Street* 30 (May 13, 1922):9–10.

451 ———. "Conquering An American Nile." *Nation's Business*, August 1922, pp. 9–11.

452 Downes, Charles. "Hoover Explains Simplified Practice." *Hardware Age*, October 5, 1922, pp. 51–53.

453 Bullard, Arthur. "Industry: The Peace Builder." *Our World*, June 1923, pp. 17–21.

454 Glover, Katherine. "A Little Child Shall Lead." *Good Housekeeping*, June 1923, pp. 121–122+. (Article begins p. 27.)

455 "Hoover Sees Prosperity in Foreign Trade: Discusses Dawes

Plan and Its Probable Effects on Business." *Printers' Ink*, September 18, 1924, pp. 37–38+.

456 Winters, S. R. "An Interview With Secretary H. C. Hoover." *Radio News*, October 1924, p. 472+.

457 Beeler, M. N. "My Plan for Eliminating Waste in the Farming Industry." *Capper's Farmer*, March 1925, p. 7+.

458 Chomel, Marie. "We the People of the United States." *Success*, January 1926, pp. 22–23+.

459 Clemens, Fred W. "Hoover Says Basic Law Governs Farming." *The Washington Farmer*, August 26, 1926, p. 3.

460 Dwyer, J. L. "Modify Anti-Trust Law Says Hoover." *Oil and Gas Journal*, October 28, 1926, p. 29.

461 Speers, L.C. "Hoover's Own Picture of Flood Tragedy." *New York Times*, May 22, 1927, section 9, p. 4+.

462 "Hoover Finds Trade with World Growing." *New York Times*, October 30, 1927, section 10, p. 2.

463 Wyckoff, C. G. "How Strong Is Our Prosperity?" *Magazine of Wall Street* 41 (November 19, 1927):99.

464 Updegraff, Robert R. "What Shall We Do With the Mississippi?" *Magazine of Business* 52 (November 1927):540–542+.

465 McIntosh, E. L. "After the Flood: An Authorized Interview with Herbert Hoover." *New York Herald Tribune Magazine*, January 29, 1928, pp. 4–5.

466 "Maintenance of Our National Industrial Progress Depends Upon Pure Science Research." *Textile World*, February 4, 1928, pp. 113–114.

467 Bennett, James O'Donnell. "Presidential Possibilities—Hoover." *Liberty*, February 11, 1928, pp. 33–34+.

468 Hard, William. "Herbert Hoover in Interview with William Hard Says America's Biggest Business is Education." *Good Housekeeping*, June 1928, p. 47+.

Also published in part as "Hoover's Faith in Education." *California Quarterly of Secondary Education*, January 1929, pp. 101–107.

469 Wright, James D. "Herbert Hoover's Business Philosophy." *Nation's Business*, September 1928, p. 14+.

470 Bunge, Alejandro. "The Hoover Idea on Argentina." *Review of River Plate*, December 21, 1928, p. 13+.

Also published in part as "No Big Brother Role for Hoover." *Literary Digest*, December 29, 1928, p. 6; "How President Hoover Views Import Need." *Forbes*, April 15, 1929, p. 38+.

471 Hunt, Frazier. "President Hoover Visions the World in Which Our Grandchildren Will Live." *Cosmopolitan*, February 1931, pp. 16–19.

472 Irwin, Will. "What America Must Do Next." *Liberty*, July 16, 1938, pp. 11–14.

473 Howard, Roy W. "Defeat of Allies Impossible, Herbert Hoover Declares, No Need for United States to Get Into War, He Says, Urging Common Sense View." *New York World Telegram*, October 3, 1939.

Also published with same title in Congressional Record. 76th Congress, second session, 1939, 85, part 1:366.

474 Woolf, S. J. "Mr. Hoover Tackles Another Relief Job." *New York Times Magazine*, January 21, 1940, p. 7+.

475 Fleming, Harold. "It Takes Time to Build a Lasting Peace." *Woman's Day*, July 1943, pp. 14–15+.

476 "The Dominant Emotion in the World Is Fear." *World Report,* May 30, 1946, pp. 28–29.

477 "How to Save Four Billions a Year." *U.S. News and World Report,* June 3, 1949, pp. 22–26.

478 "Government Is Too Big." *U.S. News and World Report,* August 5, 1955, pp. 48–52+.

Also published with same title in Addresses Upon the American Road, 1955–1960 (entry no. 40), pp. 193–214.

479 Clemens, Cyril. "My Visit With Herbert Hoover." *Hobbies,* April 1966, pp. 106–107. (Interview occurred in January 1936.)

Reports

480   United States War Department. *Report on Operations of United States Commission in Europe.* Washington, D.C.: Government Printing Office, 1914, pp. 38–44.

481   Commission for Relief in Belgium. Belgian Section. *Report Covering the Period of About Eight Months from the Inception to June 30, 1915.* London: Printed by Crowther and Goodman, 1915.

482   Commission for Relief in Belgium. *First Annual Report, November 1, 1914–October 31, 1915.* London: Printed by Crowther and Goodman, 1916. Part 1: *Provisioning Department.* Part 2: *Benevolent.* Part 3: *Financial Relief.* (Never issued.)

483   ———. *Second Annual Report, November 1, 1914–October 31, 1916.* London: Printed by Crowther and Goodman, 1917. Part 1: *Provisioning.* Part 2: *Accounts and Schedules.* Part 3: *Special Departmental Reports.* (Issued separately as entry no. 484.)

484   ———. *Special Departmental Reports from October 26, 1914, to April 1, 1917: Also Summaries from Commencement of Operations, November 1, 1914.* London: Printed by Crowther and Goodman, 1917. (Includes *Statistical Bulletin, November 1, 1916–March 25, 1917.*)

485   ———. *Third Annual Report, November 1, 1914–October 31, 1917: Provisioning.* London: Printed by Crowther and Goodman, 1918.

486   United States Food Administration. "Report to the President

on the Chicago Packing Industry, September 11, 1918." *Press Releases*, volume 14, no. 1386.

Also published with same title in The Hoover-Wilson Wartime Correspondence (entry no. 76), pp. 254–259; *Some Problems of War Readjustment* (entry no. 13), no. 4.

487 United States Congress. House. *Purchases and Disbursements Made by the United States Food Administration and by the United States Fuel Administration.* 65th Congress, second session, 1918, House Document no 890.

488 ———. *The United States Food Administration and the United States Fuel Administration for the Year 1917.* 65th Congress, second session, 1918, House Document no. 837.

489 Commission for Relief in Belgium. *Fourth Annual Report: Covering the Activities of the First Four Years, November 1, 1914–October 31, 1918: Provisioning Department.* London: Printed by Crowther and Goodman, 1919.

490 United States Congress. House. *Receipts and Expenditures* [of the American Relief Administration] *under the Act Approved February 25, 1919.* 66th Congress, second session, 1919, House Document no. 449.

491 United States Department of Labor. *Report of the Industrial Conference Called by the President, March 6, 1920.* Washington, D.C.: Government Printing Office, 1921.

492 Commission for Relief in Belgium. *Executive Personnel: Balance Sheet and Accounts, French Government Accounts, Belgian Government Accounts, Supporting Schedules; Statistical Data: Covering Six Years from Commencement of Operations, October, 1914, to September 30, 1920.* New York, 1921.

493 Conference on Unemployment, Washington, D.C., 1921. *Report of the President's Conference on Unemployment.* Washington, D.C.: Government Printing Office, 1921.

494 European Relief Council. *Interim Report, May 31, 1921.* New York: M. B. Brown Printing and Binding Company, 1921.

495 United States Department of Commerce. *Ninth Annual Report of the Secretary of Commerce, 1921.* Washington, D.C.: Government Printing Office, 1921.

496 European Relief Council. *Final Report, May 31, 1922.* New York: American Relief Administration, 1922.

497 United States Department of Commerce. *Tenth Annual Report of the Secretary of Commerce, 1922.* Washington, D.C.: Government Printing Office, 1922.

498 Colorado River Commission. *Colorado River Compact.* Washington, D.C.: Government Printing Office, 1923.

499 Inter-American High Commission. Central Executive Council. *Program of Activities of the Inter-American High Commission, October 22, 1923.* Washington, D.C., 1923. (Published in English and Spanish.)

500 United States Department of Commerce. *Eleventh Annual Report of the Secretary of Commerce, 1923.* Washington, D.C.: Government Printing Office, 1923.

501 National Conference on Street and Highway Safety, First Washington, D.C., 1924. *First National Conference on Street and Highway Safety.* Washington, D.C.,: National Capital Press, 1924.

502 "Report of the Committee appointed by the President, March 13, 1924, to Study and Make Recommendations on Matters Affecting American Merchant Marine, December 29, 1924." In *Reorganization of United States Shipping Board and United States Shipping Board Emergency Fleet Corporation: Hearing on H.R. 5369, H.R. 5395, and H.R. 8052,* issued by the United States House Committee on Merchant Marine and Fisheries, 69th Congress, first session, March 8, 1926, pp. 13–25.

503   United States Department of Commerce. *Twelfth Annual Report of the Secretary of Commerce, 1924.* Washington, D.C.: Government Printing Office, 1924.

Also published in part as "Eliminating Nation's Waste." *American Industries,* December 1924, pp. 8–9; "Herbert Hoover Makes Plea for United Workshop." *Nation's Business,* January 1925, p. 21; "Secretary of Commerce Hoover on Economic Progress." *World Almanac and Book of Facts for 1925.* New York: New York World, 1925, p. 144.

504   Commission for Relief in Belgium. *Statistical Review of Relief Operations: November 1, 1914–August 31, 1919, and to Final Liquidation,* by G. I. Gay. Stanford, California: Stanford University Press, 1925.

505   United States Department of Commerce. *Thirteenth Annual Report of the Secretary of Commerce, 1925.* Washington, D.C.: Government Printing Office, 1925.

Also published in part as Reduction of Prices Through the Elimination of Industrial Waste. Washington, D.C.: Government Printing Printing Office, 1925. (Pamphlet.) "Secretary Hoover's Economic Review of 1925." In *World Almanac and Book of Facts for 1926.* New York: New York World, 1926, pp. 154–156.

506   National Conference on Street and Highway Safety, Second, Washington, D.C., 1926. *Second National Conference on Street and Highway Safety.* Washington, D.C.: Government Printing Office, 1926.

507   United States Department of Commerce. *Fourteenth Annual Report of the Secretary of Commerce, 1926.* Washington, D.C.: Government Printing Office, 1926.

Also published in part as "Secretary Hoover Shows Progress in Elimination of Waste as Factor in American Prosperity." *Manufacturer's Record,* November 11, 1926, pp. 63–64; "Hoover on Transportation." *Traffic World* 38 (December 4, 1926):1294; *Progress in Elimination of Waste.* Washington, D.C.: Government

Printing Office, 1927. (Pamphlet.) "Secretary Hoover's Economic Review for 1926." In *World Almanac and Book of Facts for 1927.* New York: New York World, 1927, pp. 152–155.

508 United States Department of Interior. *Report of the Federal Oil Conservation Board to the President of the United States, September, 1926, Part 1,* by Hubert Work, Dwight F. Davis, and Herbert Hoover. Washington, D.C.: Government Printing Office, 1926.

509 Report on Mississippi Flood Relief Work, May 2, 1927.

Published in "Spring Floods in the Mississippi—Their Onward Sweep and Destruction." *Commercial and Financial Chronicle* 124 (May 7, 1927):2692. (Article begins p. 2687.)

510 Report to President Coolidge on Mississippi Flood Control, July 20, 1927.

Published in "Secretary Hoover Reports to President on Relief Work in Mississippi Flood." *United States Daily,* July 22, 1927, p. 5.

511 "Report on the Mississippi Flood." In *Engineers as Writers,* edited by Walter J. Miller and Leo E. A. Saidla. Freeport, New York: Books for Libraries Press, 1953, pp. 286–292.

512 United States Congress. Senate. *National Origin Provision of the Immigration Act of 1924.* 69th Congress, second session, 1927, Senate Document nos. 190 and 193. (Joint report of the Secretaries of Commerce, Labor and State.)

513 United States Department of Commerce. *Fifteenth Annual Report of the Secretary of Commerce, 1927.* Washington, D.C.: Government Printing Office, 1927.

Also published in part as "Secretary Hoover's Economic Review." In *World Almanac and Book of Facts for 1928.* New York: New York World, 1928, pp. 185–187.

514   United States St. Lawrence Commission. *St. Lawrence Water-way Project.* 69th Congress, second session, 1927, Senate Document no. 183.

515   United States Congress. Senate. *Immigration Quotas on Basis of National Origin.* 70th Congress, first session, 1928, Senate Document no. 65. (Joint report of the Secretaries of Commerce, Labor and State.)

516   United States Department of Interior. *Report II of the Federal Oil Conservation Board to the President of the United States, January, 1928,* by Hubert Work, Dwight Davis, Curtis Wilbur, and Herbert Hoover. Washington, D.C.: Government Printing Office, 1928.

517   Conference on Unemployment, Washington, D.C., 1921. Committee on Recent Economic Changes. *Recent Economic Changes in the United States.* Washington, D.C.: Government Printing Office, 1929.

Also published by McGraw Hill Book Company, New York, 1929.

518   Finnish Relief Fund, Inc. *Report to American Donors: December 1939–July 1940.* New York, (1940).

519   United States. President's Famine Emergency Committee. *Famine Report to the President (May 13, 1946).* Washington, D.C.: Government Printing Office, 1946.

Also published as "Report of Former President Hoover as to the Food Situation in Europe." In *Congressional Record.* 79th Congress, second session, 1946, 92, part 11:A2679; "World Famine." In *Addresses Upon the American Road, 1945–1948* (entry no. 32), pp. 210–220.

520   *The President's Economic Mission to Germany and Austria: Report no. 1—German Agricultural and Food Requirements, February 26, 1947.* Washington, D.C.,1947.

Also published as "Food Requirements for Germany." In *Con-*

gressional Record. 80th Congress, first session, 1947, 93, part 10:A778–781: "German Agriculture and Food Requirements." In *Addresses Upon the American Road, 1945–1948* (entry no. 32), pp. 269–285.

521 *The President's Economic Mission to Germany and Austria: Report no. 2—Austrian Agriculture and Food Requirements— Economic Reorganization, March 11, 1947.* Washington, D.C., 1947.

Also published as "On Austrian Agriculture and Food Requirements—Economic Reorganization." In *Addresses Upon the American Road, 1945–1948* (entry no. 32), pp. 294–302.

522 *The President's Economic Mission to Germany and Austria: Report no. 3—Necessary Steps for Promotion of German Exports, so as to Relieve American Taxpayers of the Burdens of Relief and for Economic Recovery of Europe (March 18, 1947).* Washington, D.C., 1947.

Also published as "Report of Honorable Herbert Hoover on Economic Mission to Germany and Austria." In *Congressional Record.* 80th Congress, first session, 1947, 93, part 10:A1207–1209; "On Necessary Steps for Promotion of German Exports so as to Relieve American Taxpayers of the Burdens of Relief and for Economic Recovery of Europe." In *Addresses Upon the American Road, 1945–1948* (entry no. 32), pp. 83–97.

523 United States Commission on Organization of the Executive Branch of the Government (1947–1949). *Budgeting and Accounting: A Report to the Congress, February, 1949.* Washington, D.C.: Government Printing Office, 1949.

524 ———. *Department of Agriculture: A Report to the Congress, February, 1949.* Washington, D.C.: Government Printing Office, 1949.

525 ———. *Foreign Affairs: A Report to the Congress, February, 1949.* Washington, D.C.: Government Printing Office, 1949.

526   ————. *General Management of the Executive Branch: A Report to the Congress, February, 1949.* Washington, D.C.: Government Printing Office, 1949.

527   ————. *National Security Organization: A Report to the Congress, February, 1949.* Washington, D.C.: Government Printing Office, 1949.

528   ————. *Office of General Services: Supply Activities: A Report to the Congress, February, 1949.* Washington, D.C.: Government Printing Office, 1949.

529   ————. *Personnel Management: A Report to the Congress, February, 1949.* Washington, D.C.: Government Printing Office, 1949.

530   ————. *The Post Office: A Report to the Congress, February, 1949.* Washington, D.C.: Government Printing Office, 1949.

531   ————. *Veteran's Affairs: A Report to the Congress, February, 1949.* Washington, D.C.: Government Printing Office, 1949.

532   ————. *Department of Commerce: A Report to the Congress, March, 1949.* Washington, D.C.: Government Printing Office, 1949.

533   ————. *Department of Interior: A Report to the Congress, March, 1949.* Washington, D.C.: Government Printing Office, 1949.

534   ————. *Department of Labor: A Report to the Congress, March, 1949.* Washington, D.C.: Government Printing Office, 1949.

535   ————. *Federal Business Enterprises: A Report to the Congress, March, 1949.* Washington, D.C.: Government Printing Office, 1949.

536 ————. *Medical Activities: A Report to the Congress, March, 1949.* Washington, D.C.: Government Printing Office, 1949.

537 ————. *Overseas Administration, Federal–State Relations, Federal Research: A Report to the Congress, March, 1949.* Washington, D.C.: Government Printing Office, 1949.

538 ————. *Regulatory Commissions: A Report to the Congress, March, 1949.* Washington, D.C.: Government Printing Office, 1949.

539 ————. *Social Security, Education, Indian Affairs: A Report to the Congress, March, 1949.* Washington, D.C.: Government Printing Office, 1949.

540 ————. *Treasury Department: A Report to the Congress, March, 1949.* Washington, D.C.: Government Printing Office, 1949.

541 ————. *Concluding Report: A Report to the Congress, May, 1949.* Washington, D.C.: Government Printing Office, 1949.

542 ————. *The Hoover Commission Report on Organization of the Executive Branch of the Government.* New York: McGraw Hill Book Company, 1949.

543 United States Commission on Organization of the Executive Branch of the Government (1953–1955). *Progress Report as of December 31, 1954: A Report to the Congress.* Washington D.C.: Government Printing Office, 1955.

544 ————. *Paperwork Management, Part 1—In the United States Government: A Report to the Congress, January, 1955.* Washington, D.C.: Government Printing Office, 1955.

545 ————. *Federal Medical Services: A Report to the Congress, February, 1955.* Washington, D.C.: Government Printing Office, 1955.

546   ———. *Personnel and Civil Service: A Report to the Congress, February, 1955.* Washington, D.C.: Government Printing Office, 1955.

547   ———. *Legal Services and Procedure: A Report to the Congress, March, 1955.* Washington, D.C.: Government Printing Office, 1955.

548   ———. *Lending Agencies: A Report to the Congress, March, 1955.* Washington, D.C.: Government Printing Office, 1955.

549   ———. *Transportation: A Report to the Congress, March, 1955.* Washington, D.C.: Government Printing Office, 1955.

550   ———. *Food and Clothing in the Government: A Report to the Congress, April, 1955.* Washington, D.C.: Government Printing Office, 1955.

551   ———. *Surplus Property: A Report to the Congress, April, 1955.* Washington, D.C.: Government Printing Office, 1955.

552   ———. *Business Enterprises: A Report to the Congress, May, 1955.* Washington, D.C.: Government Printing Office, 1955.

553   ———. *Depot Utilization — Warehousing and Storage: A Report to the Congress, May, 1955.* Washington, D.C.: Government Printing Office, 1955.

554   ———. *Research and Development in the Government: A Report to the Congress, May, 1955.* Washington, D.C.: Government Printing Office, 1955.

555   ———. *Budget and Accounting: A Report to the Congress, June, 1955.* Washington,, D.C.: Government Printing Office, 1955.

556   ———. *Business Organization of the Department of Defense: A Report to the Congress, June, 1955.* Washington, D.C.: Government Printing Office, 1955.

557 ————. *Final Report to the Congress, June, 1955.* Washington, D.C.: Government Printing Office, 1955.

558 ————. *Intelligence Activities: A Report to the Congress, June, 1955.* Washington, D.C.: Government Printing Office, 1955.

559 ————. *Overseas Economic Operations: A Report to the Congress: June, 1955.* Washington, D.C.: Government Printing Office, 1955.

560 ————. *Paperwork Management, Part 2—The Nation's Paperwork for the Government—An Experiment: A Report to the Congress, June, 1955.* Washington, D.C.: Government Printing Office, 1955.

561 ————. *Real Property Management: A Report to the Congress, June, 1955.* Washington, D.C.: Government Printing Office, 1955.

562 ————. *Water Resources and Power, vol. 1: A Report to the Congress, June, 1955.* Washington, D.C.: Government Printing Office, 1955.

563 ————. *Water Resources and Power, vol. 2: A Report to the Congress, June, 1955.* Washington, D.C.: Government Printing Office, 1955.

Testimonies

564 United States Congress. Senate. Committee on Agriculture and Forestry. *Production and Conservation of Food Supplies.* 65th Congress, first session, May 8, 1917, pp. 373–391, and May 9, 1917, pp. 411–424.

565 United States Congress. Senate. Committee on Agriculture and Forestry. *Control and Distribution of Food Supplies: Hearing on S. 2463.* 65th Congress, first session, June 19, 1917, pp. 8–60.

566 United States Congress. Senate. Subcommittee of the Committee on Manufactures. *Shortage of Sugar: Hearing on S.R. 163.* 65th Congress, second session, January 2–3, 1918, pp. 549–705.

567 United States Congress. House. Subcommittee of the Committee on Appropriations. *Urgent Deficiencies: Hearing on H.R. 9876.* 65th Congress, second session, January 31, 1918, pp. 1148–1173.

568 United States Congress. House. Committee on Agriculture. *Conservation of Foodstuffs, Feeds, Etc.: Hearing on H.R. 8717.* 65th Congress, second session, February 11, 1918, pp. 1–43.

569 United States Congress. House. Subcommittee no. 3 (Foreign Expenditures) of Expenditures in the War Department Select Committee on War Expenditures. *War Expenditures.* 66th Congress, first session, serial 4, part 12, September 2, 1919, pp. 527–560, and part 23, October 29, 1919, pp. 1223–1252.

570 United States Congress. House. Committee on Ways and Means. *Relief of European Populations.* 66th Congress, second session, January 12, 1920, pp. 57–81.

571 United States Congress. Senate. Subcommittee of the Committee on Naval Affairs. *Naval Investigation.* 66th Congress, second session, March 13, 1920, pp. 117–120.

572 United States Congress. House. Committee on the Judiciary. *Investigation of the Action of the Attorney General Relating to the Price of Louisiana Sugar: Hearing on H.R. 469.* 66th Congress, second session, May 14, 1920, pp. 287–299.

573 United States Congress. Senate. Committee on Education and Labor. *Industrial Conference.* 66th Congress, second session, May 14, 1920, pp. 25–42.

574 Statement before the Lusk Joint Legislative Investigating Committee, New York State, investigating profiteering as a cause of unrest, May 24, 1920.

Published as "Hoover on High Cost of Living." In "American Developments." *Current History* 12 (1920):567.

575 United States Congress. Senate. Select Committee on Reconstruction and Production. *Reconstruction and Production: Hearing on S.R. 350.* 66th Congress, third session, September 23, 1920, pp. 609–627.

576 United States Congress. House. Committee on Agriculture. *Future Trading.* 66th Congress, third session, January 20, 1921, pp. 895–923.

577 United States Congress. House. Committee on Ways and Means. *American Valuation.* 67th Congress, first session, May 3, 1921, pp. 41–49.

578 United States Congress. House. Committee on Interstate and Foreign Commerce. *Aids to Navigation and Pay in Lighthouse Service: Hearing on H.R. 134.* 67th Congress, first session, May 5, 1921, pp. 32–35.

579 United States Congress. House. Subcommitttee of the Committee on Appropriations. *Second Deficiency Appropriation Bill, 1921.* 67th Congress, first session, May 7, 1921, pp. 440–488.

580   United States Congress. Senate. Subcommittee of the Committee on Appropriations. *Second Deficiency Appropriation Bill, 1921: Hearing on H.R. 6300.* 67th Congress, first session, May 27, 1921, pp. 3–21.

581   United States Congress. Senate. Committee on Agriculture and Forestry. *Farmers' Export Financing Corporation: Hearing on S. 1915.* 67th Congress, first session, June 25, 1921, pp. 67–85.

582   United States Congress. House. Committee on Military Affairs. *Relief for Russian Children: Donation of Surplus Medical and Hospital Supplies of War Department for Relief of Starving Children in Volga Basin and Russian Armenia.* 67th Congress, first session, November 2, 1921, pp. 10–13.

583   United States Congress. House. Committee on Rivers and Harbors. *Pollution of Navigable Waters.* 67th Congress, second session, part 2, December 7, 1921, pp. 91–94.

584   United States Congress. House. Committee on Foreign Affairs. *Russia Relief: Hearing on H.R. 9459 and H.R. 9548.* 67th Congress, second session, December 13, 1921, pp. 37–40.

585   United States Congress. House. Committee on Interstate and Foreign Commerce. *Purchase of the Cape Cod Canal: Hearing on H.R. 9489.* 67th Congress, second session, January 9, 1922, pp. 25–31.

Also published in Purchase of the Cape Cod Canal: Hearing on H.R. 9392, issued by the House, Committee on Rivers and Harbors, 69th Congress, first session, February 9, 1926, pp. 127–133.

586   United States Congress. House. Subcommittee of the Committee on Appropriations. *Departments of Commerce and Labor Appropriation Bill, 1923.* 67th Congress, second session, January 24, 1922, pp. 4–38.

587 Statement concerning railway rate adjustments, before the Interstate Commerce Commission, Washington, D.C., February 3, 1922.

Published as, *Economic Factors in Railway Rate Adjustment*, issued by the U.S. Department of Commerce. Washington, D.C.: Government Printing Office, 1922. (Pamphlet.) *The Problem of Prosperity and the Part In It Played by the American Railroads.* New York: Reprinted by the Association of Railway Executives, 1922.

588 United States Congress. House. Committee on Foreign Affairs. *Pollution of Navigable Waters: Hearing on H.J.R. 216 and H.J.R. 297.* 67th Congress, second session, February 15, 1922, pp. 4–6.

589 United States Congress. House. Subcommittee of the Committee on Appropriations. *Third Deficiency Appropriation Bill, 1922.* 67th Congress, second session, June 14, 1922, pp. 211–214.

590 United States Congress. House. Committee on Irrigation of Arid Lands. *Protection and Development of Lower Colorado River Basin: Hearing on H.R. 11449.* 67th Congress, second session, part 1, June 21, 1922, pp. 52–62.

591 United States Congress. House. Committee on Interstate and Foreign Commerce. *Coal—Federal Fuel Distributor: Hearing on H.R. 12472.* 67th Congress, second session, August 28, 1922, pp. 15–24.

592 United States Congress. House. Subcommittee of the Committee on Appropriations. *First Deficiency Appropriation Bill, 1923.* 67th Congress, second session, September 13, 1922, pp. 11–15.

593 United States Congress. Senate. Committee on Banking and Currency. *Rural Credits.* 67th Congress, fourth session, part 6, December 30, 1922, pp. 375–384.

594 United States Congress. House. Committee on Merchant Marine and Fisheries. *To Amend the Radio Act of 1912: Hearing on H.R. 11964.* 67th Congress, fourth session, January 2, 1923, pp. 29–43.

595 United States Congress. House. Subcommittee of the Committee on Appropriations. *Third Deficiency Appropriation Bill, 1923.* 67th Congress, fourth session, February 17, 1923, pp. 489–523.

596 United States Congress. Joint Committee on the Reorganization of the Administrative Branch of the Government. *Reorganization of Executive Departments: Hearing on S.J.R. 282 of the 67th Congress.* 68th Congress, first session, January 22, 1924, pp. 327–353.

597 United States Congress. House. Committee on Rivers and Harbors. *Pollution of Navigable Waters.* 68th Congress, first session, January 23, 1924, pp. 9–16.

598 United States Congress. House. Committee on Interstate and Foreign Commerce. *To Establish in the Bureau of Foreign and Domestic Commerce of the Department of Commerce a Foreign Commerce Service of the United States: Hearing on H.R. 4517.* 68th Congress, first session, February 7, 1924, pp. 3–14.

599 United States Congress. House. Committee on Foreign Affairs. *Relief for Women and Children of Germany: Hearing on H.J.R. 180.* 68th Congress, first session, February 13, 1924, pp. 131–140.

600 United States Congress. House. Committee on Irrigation and Reclamation. *Protection and Development of Lower Colorado River Basin: Hearing on H.R. 2903.* 68th Congress, first session, part 1, February 13, 1924, pp. 28–68.

601 United States Congress. House. Committee on Merchant Marine and Fisheries. *To Regulate Radio Communication:*

Hearing on H.R. 7357. 68th Congress, first session, March 11, 1924, pp. 8–12.

602 United States Congress. House. Committee on Interstate and Foreign Commerce. *Railroad Rate Structure Survey: Hearing on H.J.R. 141.* 68th Congress, first session, April 9, 1924, pp. 45–56.

603 United States Congress. House. Committee on Military Affairs. *Universal Mobilization for War Purposes: Hearing on H.J.R. 128, H.R. 194, H.R. 4841, and H.R. 8111.* 68th Congress, first session, April 9, 1924, pp. 193–199.

Also published in Taking the Profits Out of War: Hearing on H.R. 5293. Issued by the House, Committee on Military Affairs, 74th Congress, first session, January 1935, pp. 639–645.

604 United States Congress. Senate. Committee on Interstate Commerce. *Consolidation of Railway Properties: Hearing on S. 2224.* 68th Congress, first session, May 21, 1924, pp. 14–28.

605 United States Congress. House. Committee on Interstate and Foreign Commerce. *Bureau of Civil Air Navigation in Department of Commerce: Hearing on H.R. 10522.* 68th Congress, second session, December 17, 1924, pp. 21–25.

606 United States Congress. House. Subcommittee of the Committee on Appropriations. *Department of Commerce, 1926.* 68th Congress, second session, January 5, 1925, pp. 1–6, and January 7, 1925, pp. 212–214.

607 United States Congress. House. Select Committee on Inquiry Into Operations of the United States Air Services. *Inquiry Into Operations of the United States Air Services.* 68th Congress, second session, part 2, January 10, 1925, pp. 815–821.

608 Statement concerning agricultural problems, before the President's Agricultural Commission, Washington D.C., January 19, 1925.

Published in "Secretary of Commerce Hoover in Statement to President's Agricultural Commission Urges Maintenance of Tariff, Development of Increased Consumption, Elimination of Waste." *Commercial and Financial Chronicle* 120 (January 24, 1925):411– 412.

609 United States Congress. Senate. Subcommittee of the Committee on Appropriations. *Departments of State, Justice, Commerce and Labor Appropriation Bill, 1926: Hearing on H.R. 11753.* 68th Congress, second session, January 31, 1925, pp. 39–54.

610 United States Congress. House. Committee on Interstate and Foreign Commerce. *Aircraft: Hearing Before the President's Aircraft Board.* 68th Congress, second session, September 23, 1925, pp. 318–330.

Also published as Commercial Aviation. N.p., n.d. (Pamphlet.)

611 United States Congress. Senate. Committee on Irrigation and Reclamation. *Colorado River Basin: Hearing on S.R. 320.* 69th Congress, first session, part 5, December 10, 1925, pp. 599–617.

612 United States Congress. House. Committee on Interstate and Foreign Commerce. *Crude Rubber, Coffee, Etc.: Hearing on H.R. 59.* 69th Congress, first session, January 6, 1926, pp. 1–23, and January 18, 1926, pp. 285–309.

613 United States Congress. House. Committee on Merchant Marine and Fisheries. *To Regulate Radio Communication.* 69th Congress, first session, January 6, 1926, pp. 9–15.

614 United States Congress. House. Committee on Rivers and Harbors. *Inland Waterways Systems.* 69th Congress, first session, January 30, 1926, pp. 1–22.

615 United States Congress. House. Committee on Industrial Arts and Expositions. *Sesquicentennial Exhibition, Philadelphia: Hearing on H.J.R. 144.* 69th Congress, first session, February 3, 1926, pp. 6–11.

616 United States Congress. House. Committee on Coinage, Weights and Measures. *Commission to Standardize Screw Threads: Hearing on H.R. 264.* 69th Congress, first session, February 4, 1926, pp. 3–9.

617 United States Congress. House. Committee on Foreign Affairs. *American Government Buildings and Embassy, Legation, and Consular Buildings in Foreign Countries: Hearing on H.R. 6771.* 69th Congress, first session, February 13, 1926, pp. 160–167.

618 United States Congress. House. Committee on Irrigation and Reclamation. *Colorado River Basin: Hearing on H.R. 6251 and H.R. 9826.* 69th Congress, first session, part 1, March 3, 1926, pp. 44–50.

619 United States Congress. House. Committee on Merchant Marine and Fisheries. *Reorganization of United States Shipping Board and United States Shipping Board Emergency Fleet Corporation: Hearing on H.R. 5369, H.R. 5395, and H.R. 8052.* 69th Congress, first session, March 8, 1926, pp. 13–25.

620 United States Congress. Joint Committee on Muscle Shoals. *Leasing of Muscle Shoals: Hearing on S.Con.R. 4.* 69th Congress, first session, March 27, 1926, pp. 103–114.

621 United States Congress. House. Committee on Mines and Mining. *Authorizing Investigation to Determine Location and Extent of Potash Deposits or Occurrence in United States: Hearing on S. 1821.* 69th Congress, first session, April 29, 1926, pp. 2–7.

622 United States Congress. House. Committee on Interstate and Foreign Commerce. *Coal.* 69th Congress, first session, May 14, 1926, pp. 525–542.

623 United States Congress. House. Committee on the Judiciary. *To Amend Webb-Pomerene Act.* 70th Congress, first session, January 19, 1928, pp. 20–22.

624 United States Congress. Senate. Committee on Commerce. *Flood Control.* 70th Congress, first session, part 3, February 24, 1928, pp. 681–693.

625 United States Congress. Senate. Special Committee Investigating Presidential Campaign Expenditures. *Presidential Campaign Expenditures: Hearing on S.R. 214.* 70th Congress, first session, May 9, 1928, pp. 45–66.

626 Statement for the trustees of Stanford University at a hearing on investment policy, before the San Jose Superior Court, San Jose, California, February 10, 1936.

Published in "Inflation Menace Target on Hoover." *New York Times,* February 11, 1936, p. 14.

627 United States Congress. Senate. Committee on Banking and Currency. *Emergency Price Control Act: Hearing on H.R. 5990.* 77th Congress, first session, December 16, 1941, pp. 409–427.

Also published as "Organization of War Economic Controls." In *Addresses Upon the American Road, 1941–1945* (entry no. 31), pp. 147–159.

628 United States Congress. Senate. Subcommittee of the Committee on Appropriations. *Investigation of Manpower.* 78th Congress, first session, part 1, February 8, 1943, pp. 223–244.

Also published as "Criticism of Present Manpower Policy." *Congressional Digest* 22 (March 1943):95–96; "Food Production, Manpower, Machinery." In *Addresses Upon the American Road, 1941–1945* (entry no. 31), pp. 196–99.

629 United States Congress. Senate. Subcommittee of the Committee on Foreign Relations. *Relief for Starving Peoples of Europe: Hearing on S.R. 100.* 78th Congress, first session, November 4, 1943, pp. 2–52.

Also published with same title in, Addresses Upon the American Road, 1941–1945 (entry no. 31), pp. 353–356.

630 United States Congress. House. Committee on Foreign Affairs. *Relief Assistance to Countries Devastated by War: Hearing on H.J.R. 134.* 80th Congress, first session, February 28, 1947, pp. 53–62.

Also published as "On Relief Assistance to Countries Devastated by War." In *Addresses Upon the American Road, 1945–1948* (entry no. 32), pp. 286–293.

631 United States Congress. House. Subcommittee of the Committee on Appropriations. *First Deficiency Appropriation Bill for 1947: Hearing on H.R. 2849.* 80th Congress, first session, March 19, 1947, pp. 863–881.

632 United States Congress. House. Subcommittee of the Committee on Appropriations. *Supplemental Appropriation Bill for 1948: Hearing on H.R. 4269.* 80th Congress, first session, May 27, 1947, pp. 402–423.

633 United States Congress. Senate. Subcommittee of the Committee on Foreign Relations. *St. Lawrence Seaway Project: Hearing on S.J.R. 111.* 80th Congress, first session, May 28, 1947, pp. 5–7.

634 United States Congress. Senate. Subcommittee of the Committee on Post Office and Civil Service. *Compensation of Top Government Officials.* 80th Congress, second session, December 14, 1948, pp. 53–58.

635 United States Congress. House. Committee on Expenditures in the Executive Office. *Reorganization of Government Agencies: Hearing on H.R. 1569.* 81st Congress, first session, January 31, 1949, pp. 133–158.

Also published as "On Expenditures in the Executive Office." In *Addresses Upon the American Road, 1948–1950* (entry no. 33), pp. 137–141.

636 United States Congress. Senate. Committee on Expenditures in Executive Departments. *Reorganization Act of 1949: Hear-*

ing on S. 526. 81st Congress, first session, February 7, 1949, pp. 68–84.

637   United States Congress. Senate. Committee on Armed Services. *National Security Act Amendments of 1949: Hearing on S. 1269 and S. 1843.* 81st Congress, first session, April 11, 1949, p. 127.

Also published as "On the National Security." In *Addresses Upon the American Road, 1948–1950* (entry no. 33), pp. 122–127.

638   United States Congress. House. Committee on Armed Services. *To Convert the National Military Establishment into an Executive Department of the Government, to be Known as the Department of Defense, To Provide the Secretary of Defense with Appropriate Responsibility and Authority, and with Civilian and Military Assistants Adequate to Fulfill His Enlarged Responsibility.* 81st Congress, first session, June 29, 1949, pp. 2715–2729.

Also published as part of "On the National Security." In *Addresses Upon the American Road, 1948–1950* (entry no. 33), pp. 128–131.

639   United States Congress. Senate. Committee on Expenditures in the Executive Departments. *Reorganization Plans of 1949.* 81st Congress, first session, June 30, 1949, pp. 19–38.

640   United States Congress. Senate. Subcommittee on Post Office and Civil Service. *Bills to Implement Recommendations of the Commission on Organization of the Executive Branch of the Government (The Hoover Commission): Hearing on S. 2027, S. 2062, S. 2111, S. 2212, S. 2213, S. 2509, S. 3829, and S. 3830.* 81st Congress, first session, June 30, 1949, pp. 4–11.

Also published as "Reorganization of Post Office and Civil Service." In *Addresses Upon the American Road, 1948–1950* (entry no. 33), pp. 153–154.

641   United States Congress. House. Committee on Armed Services. *National Defense Program—Unification and Strategy.* 81st Congress, first session, October 21, 1949, pp. 635–638.

Also published as part of "On the National Security." In *Addresses Upon the American Road, 1948–1950* (entry no. 33), pp. 132–136.

642 United States Congress. Senate. Committee on Expenditures in the Executive Departments. *To Improve Budgeting, Accounting and Auditing Methods of the Federal Government: Hearing on S. 2054 and Amendments.* 81st Congress, second session, March 7, 1950, pp. 217–232.

643 United States Congress. Senate. Committee on Foreign Relations and Committee on Armed Services. *Defense of Europe: Hearing on S.Con.R. 8.* 82nd Congress, first session, February 27, 1951, pp. 720–744.

Also published with same title in Forty Key Questions (entry no. 35), pp. 77–87; "On Defense of Europe." In *Addresses Upon the American Road, 1950–1955* (entry no. 38), pp. 23–41.

644 United States Congress. Senate. Committee on Banking and Currency. *Reconstruction Finance Act Amendments on 1951: Hearing on S. 514, S. 515, S. 1116, S. 1123, S. 1329, S. 1376, and S.J.R. 44.* 82nd Congress, first session, April 30, 1951, pp. 89–125.

Also published as "The Reconstruction Finance Corporation." In *Addresses Upon the American Road, 1950–1955* (entry no. 38), pp. 217–223.

645 United States Congress. House. Select Committee to Investigate the Incorporation of the Baltic States into the U.S.S.R. *Baltic States Investigation: Hearing Under Authority of H.R. 346.* 83rd Congress, first session, December 5, 1953, pp. 215–222.

646 United States Congress. Senate. Subcommittee of the Committee on Foreign Relations. *Review of the UN Charter.* 84th Congress, first session, part 12, April 21, 1955, pp. 1741–1753.

647 United States Congress. House. Subcommittee of the Committee on Government Operations. *Commission on Organization of the Executive Branch of the Government (Lending Agencies Report)*. 84th Congress, first session, June 20, 1955, p. 18.

648 United States Congress. Senate. Subcommittee on Reorganization of the Committee on Government Operations. *Administrative Vice-President*. 84th Congress second session, January 16, 1956, pp. 7–20.

Also published as "On the Proposal for an Administrative Vice-President." In *Addresses Upon the American Road, 1955–1960* (entry no. 40), pp. 221-230.

649 United States Congress. House. Special Subcommittee to Study Presidential Inability of the Committee on the Judiciary. *Presidential Inability*. 84th Congress, second session, April 11, 1956, pp. 1–2.

Addresses

1909

650 Remarks before a meeting of stockholders of the Zinc Corporation, London, England, July 1909.

Published in "Elmore Process As Applied by Zinc Corporation." *Engineering and Mining Journal* 88 (July 1909):205–206.

1917

651 Address before the New York City Rocky Mountain Club, New York City, January 29, 1917.

Published in "Belgium and Rocky Mountain Club." *Journal of American History* 11 (October 1917):575–576; *Proceedings at Reception and Dinner to Herbert Clark Hoover by Rocky Mountain Club.* N.p., n.d., pp. 2–7. (Pamphlet.)

652 Address before the Chamber of Commerce of New York State, New York City, February 1, 1917.

Published as "America's Obligations in Belgian Relief." *New York Chamber of Commerce Monthly Bulletin*, February 1917, pp. 28–37. (Reprinted as pamphlet with same title.)

653 Address at Brown University, Providence, Rhode Island, May 20, 1917.

Published as "This Year We Are Faced with a World Food Shortage." *United States Food Administration Bulletin*, no. 1 (1917), pp. 28–29.

654 Address at commencement exercises, Harvard University, Cambridge, Massachusetts, June 21, 1917.

Published as "This Is a Problem Greater Than War: It Is a Problem of Humanity." *United States Food Administration Bulletin,* no. 1 (1917), pp. 30–32.

655 Address before the Editorial Conference of Business Papers, Washington, D.C., July 21, 1917.

Published as "Conserving the Food Supply." *Engineering and Mining Journal* 104 (July 1917):125–127.

656 Address at the Smithsonian Institution, Washington, D.C., August 28, 1917.

Published as "Food Armies of Liberty." *National Geographic* 32 (September 1917):187–196; "The World's Food Shortage." *United States Food Administration Bulletin,* no. 7 (1917), pp. 10–15.

657 Address before the National Chamber of Commerce Convention, Atlantic City, New Jersey, September 19, 1917.

Published as "Weapon of Food." *National Geographic* 32 (September 1917):197–212; "From Bottom Up or Top Down?" *Nation's Business,* October 1917, pp. 22–24; "Food Administration." *United States Food Administration Bulletin,* no. 7 (1917), pp. 3–9.

Published in part as "Food Will Win the War." *Independent* 92 (December 15, 1917):510.

658 Address before the Food Conference of the Pennsylvania Public Safety Committee, Philadelphia, Pennsylvania, September 29, 1917.

Published as Address as United States Food Administrator, Washington, D.C., Delivered at the Food Conference of the Committee of Public Safety for the Commonwealth of Pennsylvania.... Philadelphia: Department of Food Supply, 1917. (Pamphlet.)

659 Address before the American Public Health Association, Washington, D.C., October 19, 1917.

Published as "Food Conservation and the War." *American Journal of Public Health* 7 (November 1917):922–927.

1918

660 Address before a meeting of hotel men, Washington, D.C., March 29, 1918.

Published as "Press Release no. 790." *United States Food Administration Press Releases*, volume 8 (1918).

661 Address before the Pittsburgh Press Club, Pittsburgh, Pennsylvania, April 18, 1918.

Published as "Food Control: A War Measure." *United States Food Administration Bulletin*, no. 15 (April 1918):1–13; "Food Control." *Journal of Home Economics* 10 (June 1918):245–254; "Some Phases of the War Food Problem." *American Medicine*, June 1918, pp. 331–335; "Food Control Is A War Measure." *United States Food Administration Bulletin*, no. 16 (July 1918):5–15; *Food in War*. London: W. H. Smith and Sons, 1918. (Pamphlet.)

662 Address before the Conference of Representatives of the Grain Trade of the United States with the Food Administration Grain Corporation, New York City, April 30, 1918.

Published as "Wheat Problems of Last Year's Harvest." *Northwestern Miller* 114 (June 12, 1918):851–852+; *America's Grain Trade: The Problem of the 1917 Harvest and Protecting the U.S.A. Domestic Situation and Effective Aid to America's Allies*. N.p., 1918. (Pamphlet.)

663 Address before the National Milk and Dairy Farm Exposition, New York City, May 23, 1918.

Published as The Dairy and the World Food Problem. Washington, D.C.: United States Food Administration, 1918. (Pamphlet.)

664 Address at Mansion House, London, England, July 23, 1918.

Published in part in "H. C. Hoover in London Speech Declares All

Anxiety as to Food Requirements in Past." *Commercial and Financial Chronicle* 107 (July 27, 1918):352-353.

665   Address before the Conference of Federal Food Administrators, Washington, D.C., November 12, 1918.

Published as Food Conservation for World Relief. Washington, D.C.: United States Food Administration, 1918. (Pamphlet.)

Published in part as "For the Homemaker: The Present Food Situation." *Journal of Home Economics* 10 (1918):513–514.

1919

666   Address at the dedication of Mesves Cemetery, France, April 27, 1919.

Published as "Hoover Dedicates the Largest American Cemetery in France." *Stanford Illustrated Review* 20 (May 1919):407.

667   Address before the American Institute of Mining and Metallurgical Engineers, New York City, September 16, 1919.

Published as "Since the Armistice." *Nation's Business,* November 1919, pp. 11–12+; "Safety of Newborn Democracies." *Forum* 62 (December 1919):551–562; "The Paramount Business of Every American Today." *System* 38 (July 1920):23.

Published in Some Problems of War Readjustment (entry no. 13), no. 1.

668   Address before the students of Stanford University, Palo Alto, California, October 2, 1919.

Published as "Our Responsibility." *Sunset,* November 1919, p. 14–16+; *The League of Nations.* San Francisco: League to Enforce Peace, 1919. (Pamphlet.) *Treaty of Peace and the League of Nations....* Boston: League for Permanent Peace, 1919. (Pamphlet.) *We Cannot Fiddle While Rome Burns.* New York: League to Enforce Peace, 1919. (Pamphlet.)

669 Address before the San Francisco Commercial Club, San Francisco, California, October 9, 1919.

Published as Mr. Hoover's Address Before the San Francisco Commercial Club. . . . New York: N.p., 1919. (Pamphlet.) The World Economic Situation. . . . San Francisco: N.p., 1919.

670 Address before the Commonwealth Club, San Francisco, California, October 15, 1919.

Published as "Address of Honorable Herbert C. Hoover." *Transactions of the Commonwealth Club of California* 14 (November 1919):434–444.

671 Address before the Rocky Mountain Club, New York City, October 27, 1919.

Published in Rocky Mountain Club: Addresses Given at Rocky Mountain Club Dinner on the Anniversary of Theodore Roosevelt's Birthday. N.p., n.d., pp. 15–17. (Pamphlet.)

672 Address before the Buffalo Chamber of Commerce, Buffalo, New York, November 12, 1919.

Published as Mr. Hoover's Address Before the Buffalo Chamber of Commerce. . . . N.p., n.d. (Pamphlet.)

673 Address before the Polish Conference, Buffalo, New York, November 12, 1919.

Published as Address of Herbert Hoover, Before the Polish Convention at Buffalo. . . . Chicago: National Polish Committee of America, 1919. (Pamphlet.)

674 Address before the Associated Charities of San Francisco, San Francisco, California, December 29, 1919.

Published as Child Welfare. . . . California Dairy Council, 1919. (Pamphlet.) Mr. Hoover's Address Before the Associated Charities of San Francisco. . . . New York, 1919. (Pamphlet.) "Unto the Least of These." *Sunset,* February 1920, p. 24+.

1920

675 Address before the American Institute of Mining and Metallurgical Engineers, New York City, February 17, 1920.

Published as "Hoover Outlines His National Policy." *Business Digest*, February 24, 1920, p. 253; "Report of the Institute Banquet, Hoover's Speech." *Engineering and Mining Journal* 109 (February 1920):497–500; "Herbert Hoover Addresses Mining Engineers." *Mechanical Engineering* 42 (March 1920):194; "Only Way Out." *Mining and Metallurgy*, March 1920, pp. 3–7.

Published in Some Problems of War Readjustment (entry no. 13), part 2.

Published in part as "Hoover—On Engineer's Interest in Public Questions." *Engineering News Record* 84 (February 26, 1920): 418–420.

676 Address at Johns Hopkins University, Baltimore, Maryland, February 23, 1920.

Published as "Hoover Declares for Treaty Compromise." *Northwestern Miller* 121 (March 3, 1920):1053–1054; *Mr. Hoover's Address at Johns Hopkins University.* . . . N.p., n.d. (Pamphlet.)

677 Address before the Western Society of Engineers, Chicago, Illinois, February 28, 1920.

Published as "Speech by Mr. Hoover Before the Western Society of Engineers." *Mining and Scientific Press* 120 (March 13, 1920): 383–386; *Mr. Hoover's Address Before the Western Society of Engineers at* . . . . N.p., n.d. (Pamphlet.)

678 Address before the Boston Chamber of Commerce, Boston, Massachusetts, March 24, 1920.

Published in "Hoover on Industrial Relations." *Industrial Management* 59 (May 1920):345–347; *Some Problems of War Readjustment* (entry no. 13), part 3.

Published as Mr. Hoover's Address Before the Boston Chamber of Commerce. . . . N.p., n.d. (Pamphlet.)

679 Address at the Northwestern Miller dinner, Minneapolis, Minnesota, August 21, 1920.

Published in "Dinner in Honor of Mr. Hoover." *Northwestern Miller* 123 (August 25, 1920):912–913.

680 Address before the American Institute of Mining Engineers, Minneapolis, Minnesota, August 26, 1920.

Published as "Mr. Hoover's Address." *Engineering and Mining Journal* 110 (September 4, 1920):453–455; "Nationalized Power." *Nation*, September 18, 1920, pp. 318–319; "National Program for Great Engineering Problem." *Mining and Metallurgy*, October 1920, pp. 3–5.

681 Address at the Lafayette–Marne celebration, U.S. Military Academy, West Point, New York, September 6, 1920.

Published as "Address of Herbert Hoover." In *Lafayette–Marne Day.* . . . United States Military Academy (1920), pp. 10–13. (Pamphlet.)

682 Address before the National Convention of the American Association of the Baking Industry, Atlantic City, New Jersey, September 22, 1920.

Published as "Herbert Hoover Praises the Bakers." *Baker's Weekly*, September 25, 1920, pp. 81–82; "The Farmer and the Price of Bread." *Baker's Helper*, October 1, 1920, pp. 1876–1877.

683 Address before the Columbia Club of Indianapolis, Indiana, October 9, 1920.

Published in part as "Hoover Says Party is For a League: Deserves Trust." *New York Times*, October 10, 1920, p. 1.

684 Address before the American Child Hygiene Association, St. Louis, Missouri, October 11, 1920.

Published by American Relief Administration.

Published as "Child Problem in America." *League of Red Cross*

Societies Bulletin 2 (January 1921):154–156; "A Program for American Children." *A.R.A. Bulletin,* no. 3, second series (November 1, 1922), pp. 1–6.

685 Address before the Farmer's Cooperative Association, Topeka, Kansas, October 13, 1920.

Published in part in "Herbert Hoover and the Federal Farm Board Project, 1921–1925," by James H. Shideler. *Mississippi Valley Historical Review* 62 (March 1956):710–729.

686 Address before the Canadian Red Cross, Toronto, Canada, October 16, 1920.

Published as "Mr. Hoover's Address." *Canadian Red Cross Society: British Empire War Relief Fund.* N.p., n.d., pp. 8–12. (Pamphlet.)

687 Address before the Federated American Engineering Societies, Washington, D.C., November 19, 1920.

Published as "Engineer's Relation to Our Industrial Problems." *Engineering News Record* 85 (November 25, 1920):1053–1055; "Engineers and Public Service." *Chemical and Metallurgical Engineering* 23 (December 1, 1920):1077–1080; "Great Area of Common Concern Between Engineers, Employer and Employees." *Mining and Metallurgy,* December 1920, pp. 3–7; "Plea for Cooperation." *American Federationist* 28 (January 1921):35–40.

688 Address at Boston, Masachusetts, December 4, 1920.

Published as "Saving the Childhood of Europe." *Federal Council Bulletin,* January 1920, pp. 20–22.

689 Address before the American Banker's Association, Chicago, Illinois, December 10, 1920.

Published in part in Memoirs, volume 2 (entry no. 11), pp. 13–14.

690 Address at the Invisible Guest Dinner, New York City, December 29, 1920.

Published by American Relief Administration.

Published as "America's Welcome to Its Invisible Guests." *A.R.A. Bulletin*, no. 8, second series (January 15, 1921), pp. 2–3.

1921

691 Address at Boston, Massachusetts, January 13, 1921.

Published as "Central European Relief." *International Conciliation*, no. 160 (March 1921), pp. 107–110.

692 Address before the Merchant's Association of New York, New York City, January 24, 1921.

Published as "Mr. Hoover Speaks." *Greater New York*, January 24, 1921, pp. 3–5.

693 Address before the American Engineering Council, Syracuse, New York, February 14, 1921.

Published as "To Check Our Industrial Waste." *Nation's Business*, April 1921, p. 34.

694 Address before the American Institute of Mining Engineers, New York City, February 16, 1921.

Published in part in "Engineering Lifted from Back Room of Blueprints to First Order of National Importance." *Mining and Metallurgy*, March 1921, pp. 17–19.

695 Address before the Public Ledger Peace Forum, Academy of Music, Philadelphia, Pennsylvania, April 15, 1921.

Published as "The Economic Administration During the Armistice." In *What Really Happened at Paris: The Story of the Peace Conference, 1918–1919*, edited by Edward Mandell House and Charles Seymour. New York: Charles Scribner's Sons, 1921, pp. 336–347; *The Economic Administration During the Armistice. . . .* Philadelphia, Pennsylvania, 1921. (Pamphlet.)

696 Address before the American Engineering Council, Philadelphia, Pennsylvania, April 16, 1921.

Published as "Reorganization of the Federal Government." *Mining and Metallurgy,* May 1921, pp. 9–10.

Published in part as "Problem of Reorganization of the Federal Government." *Proceedings of the Academy of Political Science in the City of New York* 9 (July 1921):449–452.

697   Address before the United States Chamber of Commerce, Atlantic City, New Jersey, April 28, 1921.

Published as "Analysis by Secretary Hoover of Problems of American Commerce and Industry." *Commerce Reports,* April 29, 1921, pp. 593–599; "What Government Can Do." *Nation's Business,* June 1921; pp. 11–13; *Problems of American Commerce and Industry: An Analysis by Secretary of Commerce,* issued by the Department of Commerce. Washington, D.C.: Government Printing Office, 1921. (Pamphlet.)

698   Address before the American Institute of Architects, Washington, D.C., May 12, 1921.

Published as "Cooperation of Department of Commerce in National Housing Problems." *Commerce Reports,* May 13, 1921, pp. 883–886.

699   Address before the National Association of Manufacturers, New York City, May 18, 1921.

Published as "Commerce." *American Industries,* June 1921, pp. 35–36.

700   Address at the New York Commercial's anniversary banquet, New York City, May 23, 1921.

Published as "Government and Business." In *Addresses Delivered at the One-Hundred and Twentieth Anniversary Dinner of the New York Commercial.* . . . N.p., n.d., pp. 15–19. (Pamphlet.)

701   Address before the Fourteenth Annual Conference on Weights and Measures, Washington, D.C., May 25, 1921.

Published as "Address by Honorable Herbert Hoover, Secretary of Commerce." In *Weights and Measures Fourteenth Annual Conference*, issued by the U.S. Bureau of Standards. Miscellaneous Publication no. 48. Washington, D.C.: Government Printing Office, 1922, pp. 79–80. (Pamphlet.)

702 Address before the National Shoe and Leather Exposition and Style Show, Boston, Massachusetts, July 12, 1921.

Published as "Problems Confronting World Trade Readjustment." *Commerce Reports*, July 13, 1921, pp. 209–216; "Problems of Trade Readjustment." *Advocate of Peace*, August 1921, pp. 294–297.

703 Address before the National Association of Real Estate Boards, Chicago, Illinois, July 15, 1921.

Published as "Constructive Forces in the Solution of the Housing Problem." *Commerce Reports*, July 16, 1921, pp. 273–278.

704 Address at the opening of the National Conference on Unemployment, Washington, D.C., September 26, 1921.

Published in Report of the President's Conference on Unemployment (entry no. 493), pp. 28–30.

Published in part as "Challenge to Our Moral and Economic System." *American Labor Legislation Review* 2 (1921):302–303.

705 Address before the American Manufacturers Export Association, New York City, October 6, 1921.

Published in part in "Secretary Hoover Would Have Banks of Issue Take Steps Toward Stabilization of Currencies." *Commercial and Financial Chronicle* 113 (October 29, 1921):1823–1824.

706 Remarks at the closing of the National Conference on Unemployment, Washington, D.C., October 13, 1921.

Published in Report of the President's Conference on Unemployment (entry no. 493), pp. 34–35.

707   Address before the Academy of Political Science, New York City, November 4, 1921.

Published as "Value of Good Will and Cooperation in Industry." *Proceedings of the Academy of Political Science in the City of New York* 9 (January 1922):633–635.

708   Address before the Brick Maker's Conference, Washington, D.C., November 15, 1921.

Published in part as "Excerpts from Keynote Address." In *Paving Bricks,* issued by the United States Bureau of Standards. Simplified Practice Recommendation no. 1. Washington, D.C.: Government Printing office, 1922, pp. 5–6. (Cover title: *Elimination of Waste: Simplified Practice: Paving Bricks.*) (Pamphlet.)

1922

709   Address before the American Engineering Council, Washington, D.C., January 5, 1922.

Published as "Herbert Hoover Emphasizes Duty of Engineers in Re-establishing Economic Balance." *Mechanical Engineering* 44 (March 1922):206–207.

710   Address before the Union League Club of Chicago, Chicago, Illinois, February 22, 1922.

Published as "World's Gain from Washington Conference." *Commerce Reports,* February 27, 1922, pp. 479–481.

711   Address before the Colorado River Commission, Denver, Colorado, April 1, 1922.

Published in part as "Colorado River Development." *Industrial Management* 63 (May 1922):291.

712   Address before the National Federation of Construction Industries, Chicago, Illinois, April 4, 1922.

Published in part in "Secretary Hoover Says Construction Industries Need Cleaning." *Commercial and Financial Chronicle* 114 (April 22, 1922):1727–1728.

713 Address before the Trade Association Conference, Washington, D.C., April 12, 1922.

Published in "Conference of Trade Associations Held in Washington." *Commercial and Financial Chronicle* 114 (April 22, 1922): 1726–1727.

Published as "Field and Functions of Trade Associations in American Industries." *Chemical Age* 30 (May 1922):193–195.

714 Address before the National Association of Manufacturers, New York City, May 10, 1922.

Published in part in "The Trade Associations." *American Industries*, June 1922, p. 17.

715 Address before the Russell Sage Foundation, New York City, May 10, 1922.

Published in pamphlet Plan of New York and Its Environs—The Meeting of May 10, 1922. New York: Russell Sage Foundation, 1922, pp. 11–12. (Pamphlet.)

716 Address before the Conference on Bedsteads, Springs and Mattresses, Washington, D.C., May 15, 1922.

Published in part in Bedsteads, Springs and Mattresses, issued by the United States Bureau of Standards. Simplified Practice Recommendation, no. 2. Washington, D.C.: Government Printing Office, 1922, pp. 5–6. (Cover title: *Elimination of Waste: Simplified Practice: Bedsteads, Springs and Mattresses.*) (Pamphlet.)

717 Address before the United States Section of the International Chamber of Commerce, Washington, D.C., May 15, 1922.

Published by American Relief Administration.

Published as "Russia an Economic Vacuum." *Nation's Business*, June 5, 1922 (extra edition), pp. 14–16; "American Relations to

Russia." *A.R.A. Bulletin*, no. 25, second series (June 19, 1922), pp. 2–6.

718 Address before the National Chamber of Commerce of the United States, Washington, D.C., May 16, 1922.

Published as "Year of Cooperation." *Nation's Business*, June 5, 1922 (extra edition), pp. 12–14.

719 Address before the Fifteenth Annual Conference on Weights and Measures, Washington, D.C., May 24, 1922.

Published as "Address by Herbert Hoover, Secretary of Commerce." In *Weights and Measures Fifteenth Annual Conference*, issued by the United States Bureau of Standards. Miscellaneous Publication no. 51. Washington, D.C.: Government Printing Office, pp. 25–26. (Pamphlet.)

720 Address before the National Conference on Social Work, Providence, Rhode Island, June 27, 1922.

Published as "Some Human Wastes of Industry." *Survey* 48 (July 15, 1922):505–506; "Waste of Human Effort in Industry." *Proceedings of the National Conference of Social Work, 1922*, pp. 64–67.

721 Address before the Salesmen's Association of the American Chemical Industry, New York City, September 12, 1922.

Published in part in "Secretary Hoover Says Public Interest is Paramount in Coal Industry." *Commercial and Financial Chronicle* 115 (September 16, 1922):1278–1279; "Public and Coal Industry." *Commerce Reports*, September 18, 1922, pp. 1278–1279.

722 Address before the American Child Hygiene Association, Washington, D.C., October 12, 1922.

Published as "Presidential Address Before the American Child Hygiene Association." *A.R.A. Bulletin*, no. 30, second series (November 1922), pp. 1–3; (Published by American Relief Administration); "Presidential Address." *Transactions of the American Child Hygiene Association* 13 (1922):13–17.

723   Address at Toledo, Ohio, October 16, 1922.

Published in "Herbert Hoover on Repayment of European Debts to United States." *Commercial and Financial Chronicle* 115 (October 21, 1922):1780–1781.

Published as "Repayment of European Debts to Our Government." *International Conciliation*, no. 181 (December 1922), pp. 163–171.

724   Address at Grand Rapids, Michigan, October 17, 1922.

Published as "Eighteen Months of Business in Government." *American Industries*, January 1923, pp. 21–22.

Published in part in "Secretary Hoover on Economics and Accomplishments of Harding Administration." *Commercial and Financial Chronicle* 115 (November 11, 1922):2109–2110.

725   Address before the Chamber of Commerce, Detroit, Michigan, October 17, 1922.

Published in "Proposal by Herbert Hoover for Reserve Bank of Railway Rolling Stock." *Commercial and Financial Chronicle* 115 (November 11, 1922):2124–2125.

726   Address before the San Francisco Chamber of Commerce, San Francisco, California, November 29, 1922.

Published as "Our Economic Situation, Transportation and the Colorado River Project." *San Francisco Business* (San Francisco Chamber of Commerce), December 8, 1922, p. 17.

727   Address before the Commonwealth Club of California, San Francisco, California, December 1, 1922.

Published as "Address by Secretary Hoover." *Transactions of the Commonwealth Club of California* 17 (December 1922):450–458.

728   Address at the unveiling of the Isis Statue, Stanford University, Palo Alto, California, December 4, 1922.

Published as "Isis." *Commission for Relief in Belgium Bulletin*, no. 11 (April 4, 1923), p. 18. (Article begins on p. 17.) (Published by Commission for Relief in Belgium.)

729 Address at Phoenix, Arizona, December 8, 1922.

Published as The Colorado River Pact. N.p., n.d. (Pamphlet.)

1923

730 Address before the Metropolitan Managers, New York City, January 27, 1923.

Published in Addresses Delivered at the Triennial Conventions, Manager's Annual Banquets and at Miscellaneous Gatherings of the Metropolitan Life Insurance Co. New York: Metropolitan Life Insurance Co., 1928, pp. 181–184. (Pamphlet.)

731 Address before the National League of Women Voters, Des Moines, Iowa, April 11, 1923.

Published as "Address by Secretary of Commerce before the Annual Convention of the National League of Women Voters." *International Conciliation*, no. 186 (1923), pp. 136–145; "America's Next Step." In *The World Court*, by Warren G. Harding, Charles Evans Hughes, Elihu Root, John Hessin Clarke, Herbert Hoover, and Edward Mandell House. Boston: World Peace Foundation, 1923, pp. 61–68. (A World Peace Foundation Pamphlet.)

732 Address before the Chamber of Commerce of the United States, New York City, May 8, 1923.

Published as "We Can Hold the Prosperity We Have." *Nation's Business*, June 5, 1923 (extra edition), pp. 11–13; *Address of Secretary Hoover Before the Chamber of Commerce of the United States, 11th Annual Meeting.* . . . Washington, D.C., 1923. (Pamphlet.)

733 Address before the National Conference of Social Work, Washington, D.C., May 18, 1923.

Published as "Informal Remarks." *Proceedings of the National Conference of Social Work, 1923*, pp. 98–103.

734 Address before the Sixteenth Annual Conference on Weights and Measures, Washington, D.C., May 23, 1923.

Published as "Address by Secretary of Commerce, Honorable Herbert Hoover." In *Weights and Measures Sixteenth Annual Conference*, issued by the United States Bureau of Standards. Miscellaneous Publication no. 55. Washington, D.C.: Government Printing Office, 1923, pp. 76–81. (Pamphlet.)

735 Address before the State Purchasing Agents of the Department of Commerce, Washington, D.C., May 26, 1923.

Published in part as "Industrial Standarization." In *Scientific Management Since Taylor*, edited by Edward Eyre Hunt. New York: McGraw Hill Book Company, 1924, pp. 189–193.

736 Address before the World Dairy Congress, Washington, D.C., October 2, 1923.

Published as "Dairy Products' Place in Improvement of Human Health." *Proceedings of the World Dairy Congress, 1923*, pp. 14–17; *Dairy Products' Place in Improvement of Human Health*, issued by the United States Animal Industry Bureau. Washington, D.C.: Government Printing Office, 1924. (Pamphlet.)

737 Address before the Superpower Conference, New York City, October 13, 1923.

Published as "Secretary of Commerce Herbert Hoover on Purpose of Superpower Conference." *Commercial and Financial Chronicle* 117 (October 20, 1923):1742–1743.

Published in part as "For Superpower Development and Control." *American City* 29 (November 1923):525.

738 Address before the American Child Health Association, Detroit, Michigan, October 15, 1923.

Published as "Address of Honorable Herbert Hoover as President of American Child Health Association." *Mother and Child* 4 (November 1923):483–486; "Address." *Transactions of the American Child Health Association* 1 (1923):11–14.

739   Address before the Investment Banker's Association, Washington, D.C., October 30, 1923.

Published as "Herbert Hoover, While Conceding Loan of Surplus Capital Abroad Is Necessary, Says Moneys Should Not Be Dissipated in Military Expenditures." *Commercial and Financial Chronicle* 117 (November 3, 1923):1940.

1924

740   Address before the Transportation Conference of the Chamber of Commerce of the United States, Washington, D.C., January 9, 1924.

Published as Address of Honorable Herbert Hoover, Secretary of Commerce, at the Transportation Conference Called by the Chamber of Commerce of the United States. . . . Washington, D.C., 1924. (Pamphlet.)

Published in part as "Transportation's Ten Commandments." *Nation's Business*, March 1924, p. 60.

741   Address before the American Engineering Council, Washington, D.C., January 10, 1924.

Published as part of "The Engineer's Place in the World." *Engineering News Record* 92 (January 24, 1924):160.

742   Address before the Second National Conference of the Izaak Walton League of America, Chicago, April 12, 1924.

Published in part as "National Policies in Fisheries." *Outdoor America*, May 1924, pp. 53–54; "Fishing for Fun." *Congressional Record*, 88th Congress, second session, 1964, 110, part 24:A1833.

743   Address before the Chamber of Commerce of the United States, Cleveland, Ohio, May 7, 1924.

Published as "Secretary Hoover on Principles of Business Conduct: Relation of Government to Business." *Commercial and Financial Chronicle* 118 (May 17, 1924):2389–2391; "If Business Doesn't

Government Will." *Nation's Business*, June 5, 1924 (extra edition), pp. 7–9; "Some Phases of the Government in Business." *Congressional Record.* 68th Congress, first session, 1924, 65, part 8:8134–8136.

744 Address by radio from Washington, D.C., to the National Electric Light Association, Atlantic City, New Jersey, May 21, 1924.

Published as "Superpower and Interconnection." *Electrical World* 83 (May 24, 1924):1078–1080.

745 Address before the Seventeenth Annual Conference on Weights and Measures, Washington, D.C., May 29, 1924.

Published as "Address by the Secretary of Commerce, Honorable Herbert Hoover." In *Weights and Measures Seventeenth Annual Conference*, issued by the United States Bureau of Standards. Miscellaneous Publication no. 59. Washington, D.C.: Government Printing Office, 1924, pp. 135–137. (Pamphlet.)

746 Address before the First World Power Conference, London, England, July 3, 1924.

Published in part as "Government Policies in Relation to Power Development." *Electric Light and Power* 8 (June 1930):31.

747 Address before the United States Fisheries Association, Atlantic City, New Jersey, September 5, 1924.

Published in part in the Twelfth Annual Report of the Secretary of Commerce (entry no. 503), pp. 25–26.

748 Address by radio from Washington, D.C., September 29, 1924.

Published as "Secretary of Commerce Hoover on Effects of Government Ownership, Proposed by Senator La Follette's Party." *Commercial and Financial Chronicle* 119 (October 25, 1924): 1917–1919; *Government Ownership.* N.p., n.d.

Published in part as "Public Ownership and the American Plan." *Electrical World* 84 (October 4, 1924):727–729. (Pamphlet.)

749   Address before the American Dairy Association, Milwaukee, Wisconsin, October 1, 1924.

Published as "Advancement of Cooperative Marketing." *Arizona Industrial Congress Bulletin,* no. 32, December 30, 1924, pp. 3–8; "Cooperative Marketing." In *Agricultural Relief: Hearings Before the Committee on Agriculture of the House of Representatives.* 68th Congress, second session, February 14, 1925, part 11:388–392.

750   Address at opening of Third National Radio Conference, Washington, D.C., October 6, 1924.

Published in "Secretary Hoover Urges Adoption of National Program in Speech Before National Radio Conference—Size of Radio Industry." *Commercial and Financial Chronicle* 119 (November 8, 1924):2136–2137.

751   Address at Norwegian Old People's Home Dedication Service, Norwood, Illinois, November 30, 1924.

Published as "Speech of Honorable Herbert Hoover, Secretary of Commerce of the United States, at Norwegian Old People's Home Dedication Service." In the *Norwegian Old People Home Society Annual Report for 1924.* N.p., (1924), pp. 23–25.

752   Address at a dinner honoring Owen D. Young, New York City, December 11, 1924.

Published as "World's Benefit from Dawes Plan and New Conception of Industrial Trusteeship." *Chemical and Metallurgical Engineering* 31 (December 22, 1924):958–959.

753   Address at the opening of the First National Conference on Street and Highway Safety, Washington, D.C., December 15, 1924.

Published as Address of Secretary Hoover Before the National Conference on Street and Highway Safety. . . . Washington, D.C., 1924. (Pamphlet.)   "Opening Address by Honorable Herbert Hoover, Secretary of Commerce and Chairman of National Conference on Street and Highway Safety." In *First National Conference on Street and Highway Safety* (entry no. 501), pp. 7–11.

754 Remarks at the closing of the First National Conference on Street and Highway Safety, Washington, D.C., December 16, 1924.

Published in First National Conference on Street and Highway Safety (entry no. 501), pp. 37–39. (Pamphlet.)

1925

755 Address before the Association of General Contractors of America, Washington, D.C., January 12, 1925.

Published as Address by Honorable Herbert Hoover, Secretary of Commerce, Delivered before the Sixth Annual Meeting of the Association of General Contractors of America.... N.p., n.d. (Pamphlet.)

756 Address before the National Distribution Conference of the Chamber of Commerce of the United States, Washington, D.C., January 14, 1925.

Published as "Yes, We Can Cut Marketing Costs." *Nation's Business*, March 1925, p. 48; *Reducing the Cost of Distribution.* Washington, D.C., 1925. (Pamphlet.) *A Problem of Distribution.* Washington, D.C., 1929. (Pamphlet.)

757 Address by telephone from Washington, D.C., to the Academy of Political Science, New York City, March 9, 1925.

Published as "The Diffusion of Property Ownership." *National Republic*, April 1925, p. 48.

758 Address before the Clay Products Institute, Washington, D.C., March 18, 1925.

Published in "Hoover Commends Clay Products Institute." *Brick and Clay Record*, March 31, 1925, p. 1.

759   Address before the American Relief Administration Association first annual reunion, New York City, March 21, 1925.

Published as "America in European Restoration." *A.R.A. Association Review* (April 1, 1925):3–5. (Published by American Relief Administration.)

760   Address before a round table conference sponsored by the National Civic Federation, New York City, April 11, 1925.

Published as "Waste In Industry." *American Federationist* 32 (June 1925):470–472; *Elimination of Industrial Waste in Its Relation to Labor.* N.p., n.d. (Pamphlet.)

Published in part as "Elimination of Industrial Waste." *National Republic*, May 1925, p. 28.

761   Address before the Associated Advertising Clubs of the World, Houston, Texas, May 11, 1925.

Published as Desire and Goodwill. N.p., n.d. (Pamphlet.) *Public Relations of Advertising.* N.p., n.d. (Pamphlet.)

762   Address before the Chamber of Commerce of the United States, Washington, D.C., May 21, 1925.

Published as "200 Bureaus, Boards and Commissions." *Nation's Business*, June 5, 1925 (extra edition), pp. 9–10; *Reduction of Waste in Government by Reorganization of Executive Departments.* N.p., n.d. (Pamphlet.)

763   Address before the Eighteenth Annual Conference on Weights and Measures, Washington, D.C., May 27, 1925.

Published as "Address by Secretary of Commerce, Honorable Herbert Hoover." In *Weights and Measures Eighteenth Annual Conference*, issued by the United States Bureau of Standards. Miscellaneous Publication no. 70. Washington, D.C.: Government Printing Office, 1925, pp. 74–77. (Pamphlet.)

764   Address at commencement exercises, Penn College, Oskaloosa, Iowa, June 12, 1925.

Published in Penn College Bulletin, July 1925, p. 1.

765 Address before the National Electric Light Association, San Francisco, California, June 17, 1925.

Published as State Versus Federal Regulation in Transformation of Power Industry to Central Generation and Interconnection of Systems. Washington, D.C., 1925. (Pamphlet.)

Published in part in "Secretary Hoover Sees No Reason for Federal Regulation of Power Systems." *Manufacturer's Record,* June 25, 1925, pp. 91–92.

766 Address before the Sacramento Chamber of Commerce, the Sacramento Retail Merchants' Association, and the Stockton Chamber of Commerce, Sacramento and Stockton, California, June 27, 1925.

Published as The Future Development of the Great Valley of California. N.p., n.d. (Pamphlet.)

767 Address before the Philadelphia Chamber of Commerce, Philadelphia, Pennsylvania, June 1925.

Published as "Interconnection Is Now Road of Electrical March to a More Economical Expansion and Development of Industry." *Philadelphia Chamber of Commerce News Bulletin,* June 1925, pp. 9–11.

768 Address before the National Association of Railroad and Utilities Commissioners, Washington, D.C., October 14, 1925.

Published as "Why Public Interest Requires State Rather than Federal Regulation of Electric Public Utilities." *Commerce Reports,* October 26, 1925, pp. 190–193; *Why the Public Interest Requires Local Rather than Federal Regulation of Electric Public Utilities.* Washington, D.C., 1925. (Pamphlet.)

769 Address before the Missouri River Improvement Conference, Kansas City, Missouri, October 19, 1925.

Published as "The Need of Inland Waterways for Agriculture and Industry." *Commerce Reports,* November 2, 1925, pp. 255–258;

Inland Waterways and Missouri River Navigation: An Address. Kansas City, Missouri: Missouri River Navigation Association, 1925. (Pamphlet.) "Our Birthright of Waterways." *National Spectator*, March 20, 1926, pp. 3–6.

770   Address before the International Convention of Young Men's Christian Associations of North America, Washington, D.C., October 26, 1925.

Published as The Mission of the Y.M.C.A. N.p., n.d. (Pamphlet.) *Published in part as* "Perils Ahead Are Moral, Not Economic." *National Republic*, December 1925, p. 16.

771   Address before the Chamber of Commerce, Erie, Pennsylvania, October 31, 1925.

Published as "Foreign Combinations to Fix Prices in Imported Raw Materials." *Commerce Reports*, November 16, 1925, pp. 378–380; "America Solemnly Warns Foreign Monopolists of Raw Materials." *Current History* 23 (December 1925):307–311; *Foreign Prices Now Fixing Prices of Raw Materials Imported Into the United States.* N.p., n.d. (Pamphlet.)

772   Address at opening of the Fourth Annual Radio Conference, Washington, D.C., November 9, 1925.

Published as "A Statement by Secretary Hoover on Radio Progress and Problems." *Telegraphy and Telephone Age* 22 (November 16, 1925):536.

Published in Spanish as "Los progresos y problemas de la radiotransmisión." In *Finanzas, industria, comercio*, no. 15, issued by the Pan American Union. March 1926.

773   Address by radio from Washington, D.C., November 12, 1925.

Published as "Secretary of Commerce Summarizes Work of Committees." *New York Herald Tribune Radio Magazine*, November 15, 1925, p. 1.

774   Address before the National Merchant Marine Conference of

the Chamber of Commerce of the United States, Washington, D.C., November 16, 1925.

Published in "Merchant Marine Conference." *Traffic World* 36 (November 21, 1925):1222–1223; *Reorganization of the United States Shipping Board and United States Emergency Fleet Corporation* (entry no. 620), pp. 74–76.

Published as A Merchant Marine Policy. N.p., n.d. (Pamphlet.)

775 Address before the American Society of Mechanical Engineers, New York City, December 1, 1925.

Published as The Vital Need for Greater Financial Support of Pure Science Research. Washington, D.C.: National Research Council, 1925. (Pamphlet); "The Value of Pure Science Research." *Manufacturer's News*, January 1926, p. 9; "The Vital Need for Greater Financial Support of Pure Science Research." *Mechanical Engineering* 48 (January 1926):6–7.

776 Address before the American Mining Congress, Washington, D.C., December 9, 1925.

Published as "Hoover Message." *Mining Congress Journal* 12 (January 1926):11–12.

777 Address before the National Rivers and Harbors Conference, Washington, D.C., December 9, 1925.

Published as "National System of Waterways." *Proceedings of the Twenty-First Convention of National Rivers and Harbors Congress....* N.p., n.d., pp. 16–23.

1926

778 Address before the Second National Conference on Outdoor Recreation, Washington, D.C., January 21, 1926.

Published as "All Men Are Equal Before Fish." *National Spectator*, March 6, 1926, pp. 10–11; "Herbert Hoover Talks About Constructive Joy." *National Parks Bulletin*, March 1926, p. 17; "Live— Don't Just Exist." *Outdoor America*, March 1926, p. 24.

779 Address before the Department of Superintendence of the National Education Association, Washington, D.C., February 25, 1926.

Published as Education As A National Asset. N.p., n.d. (Pamphlet.) *Hoover on Teaching and Education.* Washington, D.C.: Republican National Committee, 1928. (Pamphlet.)

780 Address before the John Ericsson Republican League of Illinois, Chicago, Illinois, March 9, 1926.

Published as "Hoover on Waterways." Traffic World 37 (March 13, 1926):707–708; *The Waterways Outlet from the Middle West.* Chicago Association of Commerce and the Illinois River Division of the Mississippi Valley Association, 1926. (Pamphlet.)

Published in part as "Tribute to John Ericsson." *American Scandinavian Review*, May 1926, p. 272.

781 Address before the Export Managers' Club of New York, New York City, March 16, 1926.

Published as "Secretary Hoover on Future of Foreign Trade—Control of Raw Materials by Foreign Governments." *Commercial and Financial Chronicle* 122 (March 2, 1926):1550–1551; "Future of Our Foreign Trade." *Commerce Reports*, March 22, 1926, pp. 698–702.

782 Address at the opening of the Second National Conference on Street and Highway Safety, Washington, D.C., March 23, 1926.

Published as "Opening address of the Chairman, Honorable Herbert Hoover, Secretary of Commerce." In *Second National Conference on Street and Highway Safety* (entry no. 506), pp. 7–12. (Pamphlet.)

783 Remarks at the closing of the Second National Conference on Street and Highway Safety, Washington, D.C., March 25, 1926.

Published in Second National Conference on Street and Highway Safety (entry no. 506), pp. 26–28.

784 Address before the Chamber of Commerce of the United States, Washington, D.C., May 12, 1926.

Published as "We Can Cooperate and Yet Compete." *Nation's Business,* June 5, 1926 (extra edition), pp. 11–14; *Some of the Currents of Development in American Business.* Washington, D.C., 1926. (Pamphlet.)

785 Address before the American Health Congress and the American Child Health Association, Atlantic City, New Jersey, May 18, 1926.

Published as "Our Goal, The Normal Child." *Transactions of the American Child Health Association* 3 (1926) part 3, pp. 1–6.

786 Address before the Nineteenth Annual Conference on Weights and Measures, Washington, D.C., May 27, 1926.

Published as "Address by Secretary of Commerce Honorable Herbert Hoover." In *Weights and Measures Nineteenth Annual Conference,* issued by the United States Bureau of Standards. Miscellaneous Publication no. 74. Washington, D.C.: Government Printing Office, 1926, pp. 116–118. (Pamphlet.)

787 Address at the opening of the Sesqui-Centennial Exposition, Philadelphia, Pennsylvania, May 31, 1926.

Published in part in "Opening of Sesqui-Centennial Exposition in Philadelphia—Addresses by Secretaries Kellogg and Hoover and Mayor Kendrick." *Commercial and Financial Chronicle* 122 (June 5, 1926):3162. (Article begins on p. 3161.)

788 Address at commencement exercises, "University of Georgia, Athens, Georgia, June 16, 1926.

Published as "Higher Education and State Government." *High School Quarterly,* July 1926, pp. 195–205; "Responsibilities of Our Universities." *City Builder,* July 1926, pp. 18–19; *Higher Education and State Government.* Washington, D.C., 1926. (Pamphlet.)

789   Address at the launching of the S.S. *Malolo* of Matson Navigation Company, Philadelphia, Pennsylvania, June 26, 1926.

Published as "The Malolo: A Pledge of Service." *Aloha* (Matson
Navigation Company), August 1926, p. 7–8.

790   Address before the International Association of Chiefs of Police,
Chicago, Illinois, July 19, 1926.

Published as "Address of Honorable Herbert Hoover." *Proceedings
of the International Association of Chiefs of Police, Thirty-Third
Convention, Chicago, 1926.* N.p., n.d., pp. 70–72.

791   Address before the Minneapolis Civic and Commerce Association, Minneapolis, Minnesota, July 20, 1926.

*Published as Need for Comprehensive Inland Waterway Develop-
ment.* Washington, D.C.: 1926; "Open Up Our Choked Waterways." *World Review* 3 (January 24, 1927):243.

Published in part as "Why Inland Waterways Should Be Developed." *Review of Reviews* 74 (December 1926):595–598.

792   Address before the Columbia River Basin League, Seattle,
Washington, August 21, 1926.

*Published as A National Policy in Development of Water Re-
sources.* N.p., n.d. (Pamphlet.)

Published in part as "Waterway Policy Plea." *Traffic World* 38
(August 28, 1926):482–484.

793   Address before the University Club, Los Angeles, California,
September 2, 1926.

Published as The Organization of Democracy. N.p., n.d. (Pamphlet.)

794   Address before the National Republican Club, Republican
Committee and the Republican Woman's Club, New York City,
October 16, 1926.

Published as Speech of Honorable Herbert Hoover, Secretary of Commerce, before the National Republican Club. . . . N.p., n.d. (Same address as entry no. 795.) (Pamphlet.)

795 Address at Springfield, Ohio, October 21, 1926.

Published as Speech at Springfield, Ohio. . . . Washington, D.C.: Published by author, 1926. (Same address as entry no. 794.) (Pamphlet.)

796 Address before the Mississippi Valley Association, St. Louis, Missouri, November 22, 1926.

Published in "Engineering Skill, Not Legal Controversies, Will Solve Waterways Problems, Says Mr. Hoover." *United States Daily*, November 23, 1926, p. 8.

Published as National Plan in Development of Nation's Water Resources. Mississippi Valley Association, 1926. (Pamphlet.)

797 Address on occasion of the anniversary of the United States Bureau of Standards, Washington, D.C., December 4, 1926.

Published in "Bureau of Standards is Called Greatest of all Laboratories." *United States Daily*, December 7, 1926, p. 8.

798 Address before the American Association for the Advancement of Science and the Society of Sigma Xi, Philadelphia, Pennsylvania, December 28, 1926.

Published as "The Nation and Science." *Science* 65 (January 14, 1927):26–29; "Nation and Science." *Mechanical Engineering* 49 (February 1927):137–138.

1927

799 Address before the New Haven Chamber of Commerce, New Haven, Connecticut, March 12, 1927.

Published in "Shipway Urged in St. Lawrence by Mr. Hoover." *United States Daily*, March 14, 1927, p. 1; *St. Lawrence Shipway.* N.p., n.d. (Pamphlet.)

800 Address before the American Automobile Association Conference of Club and Association Secretaries, Washington, D.C., March 23, 1927.

Published as "Address of Honorable Herbert Hoover." In *Third Conference of Club and Association Secretaries.* Washington, D.C.: American Automobile Association, 1927, pp. 47–49. (Pamphlet.)

801 Address before the Motion Picture Producers and Distributors of America and Representatives of Latin American Republics, New York City, April 2, 1927.

Published as "American Relations." *Hispania* 10 (May 1927):129–137.

Published in part as "Motion Pictures, Trade and Welfare of Our Western Hemisphere." *Advocate of Peace*, May 1927, pp. 291–292.

Published in Spanish as "El Cine como elemento de progreso." *Bulletin of the Pan American Union*, July 1927, pp. 686–694.

802 Address before the Atlantic States Shippers Regional Advisory Board, Washington, D.C., April 5, 1927.

Published in "Improvement Noted in Railway Efficiency." *United States Daily*, April 6, 1927, p. 1.

803 Address before the Izaak Walton League of America, Chicago, Illinois, April 9, 1927.

Published as A Remedy for Disappearing Game Fishes. Washington, D.C.: Government Printing Office, 1927. (Pamphlet.) *The American's Right to Fish.* Washington, D.C.: Republican National Committee, 1928. (Pamphlet.) "A Remedy for Disappearing Game Fishes." In *Hoover After Dinner* (entry no. 21), pp. 89–112; *A Remedy for Disappearing Game Fishes* (entry no. 18), pp. 3–34.

804 Address by radio from Memphis, Tennessee, April 30, 1927.

Published in "Hoover Appeals for Aid Over Radio." *New York Times*, May 1, 1927, p. 2.

805 Address before the Third Pan American Commercial Conference, Washington, D.C., May 2, 1927.

Published as "The Secretary of Commerce, Herbert C. Hoover." *Proceedings of the Third Pan American Commercial Conference, May 2–5, 1927.* Washington, D.C.: Pan American Union, 1927, pp. 43–48.

Published in part in "Secretary of Commerce Hoover at Pan-American Conference Would Confine Loans to Foreign Countries for Productive Enterprise—State Department's Position." *Commercial and Financial Chronicle* 124 (May 7, 1927):2687–2688.

806 Address before the American Child Health Association, Washington, D.C., May 9, 1927 (read by Dr. Thomas Wood).

Published in "Mr. Hoover Advocates Realization of Perfect Childhood in America." *United States Daily,* May 11, 1927, p. 4.

807 Address by radio from New Orleans, Louisiana, May 28, 1927.

Published in "Hoover Asks Nation for $2,000,000 More in Appeal by Radio." *New York Times,* March 29, 1927, p. 1.

Published as "No One Has Gone Hungry, Unclothed, Unprotected." *Red Cross Courier,* July 1, 1927, p. 20.

808 Address on occasion of "Hoover Day", Little Rock, Arkansas, June 25, 1927.

Published in "Secretary Hoover Acclaimed in Arkansas for Flood Relief Work—Declares Effects of Flood Are Passing But Deplores Second Inundation." *Commercial and Financial Chronicle* 125 (July 2, 1927):46.

Published in part in "Red Cross 'The Banner of Mercy and Skilled Protector'—Herbert Hoover." *Red Cross Courier,* August 15, 1927, p. 18.

809 Address at the opening of the International Radiotelegraph Conference, Washington, D.C., October 4, 1927.

Published in "Mr. Hoover Declares That Universal Code is Necessary to Prevent Chaos in Radio." *United States Daily*, October 5, 1927, p. 2.

Published as Address of Secretary Hoover at Opening Meeting of International Radiotelegraph Conference. Washington, D.C.: Government Printing Office, 1927. (Available in Spanish and French.) (Pamphlet.)

810   Address before the Anthracite Cooperative Congress, Mount Carmel, Pennsylvania, November 2, 1927.

Published in Journal of Proceedings—Anthracite Co-Operative Congress, November 9–10, 1927, pp. 21–24.

Published in part in "Movement by Coal Miners, Operators and Retailers for Study of Anthracite Coal Market with View to Stabilizing Industry." *Commercial and Financial Chronicle* 125 (November 26, 1927):2876.

811   Address before the Iowa Society of Washington, Washington, D.C., November 10, 1927.

Published as "Boyhood In Iowa." *Palimpsest*, July 1928, pp. 269–276; *Hoover Recalls His Iowa Boyhood Days*. Washington, D.C., Republican National Committee, 1928. (Pamphlet.) "An Informal Address by Herbert Hoover Before the Iowa Society of Washington." in *Hoover After Dinner* (entry no. 21), pp. 123–135; and in *A Boyhood in Iowa* (entry no. 19), pp. 13–26.

812   Address before the Mississippi Valley Association, St. Louis, Missouri, November 14, 1927.

Published as "Improvement of Our Mid-West Waterways." *American Academy of Political and Social Science Annals* 135 (January 1928):15–24; "Improvement of Our Mid-West Waterways." *Congressional Record*. 70th Congress, first session, 1927, 69, part 1:132–135.

813   Address at the closing of the International Radiotelegraph Conference, Washington, D.C., November 25, 1927.

Published in "Radio Convention Adopted and Signed by Representatives of Governments." *United States Daily*, November 26, 1927, p. 2.

814 Address before the American Mining Congress, Washington, D.C., December 1, 1927.

Published in "Conservation of Mine Resources Advocated by Secretary Hoover." *United States Daily*, December 2,1927, p. 11.

Published as "Economic Importance of Mining to the Nation." *Mining Congress Journal* 14 (January 1928):15.

Published in part as "Status of Mining Industries." *Engineering and Mining Journal*, December 17, 1927, p. 989.

1928

815 Address before the Citizens Conference on Community Welfare sponsored by the Association of Community Chests and Councils, Washington, D.C., February 20, 1928.

Published as "The Human Welfare Responsibilities of Community Chests." In *Citizens Conference of Community Welfare*. New York: Association of Community Chests & Councils, 1928, pp. 3–7. (Pamphlet.)

Published in part as "Community Responsibility for Human Welfare." *Red Cross Courier*, March 15, 1928, pp. 5–6.

816 Address on receiving the Saunders Mining Medal before the American Institute of Mining and Metallurgical Engineers, New York City, February 21, 1928.

Published as "Engineer's Contribution to Modern Life." *Mining and Metallurgy*, March 1928, pp. 104–105; "Engineer's Contribution to Modern Life." In *The Profession of Engineering*, edited by Dugald Jackson and W. Jones. New York: John Wiley and Sons, 1929, pp. 119–124.

817 Address by radio, sponsored by the American Child Health Association, May 1, 1928.

Published in part in "May Day on the Air—1928." *Child Health Bulletin*, May 1928, pp. 1–2.

818 Address at the National Oratorical Contest, Washington, D.C., May 26, 1928.

Published in "Mr. Hoover Defends American Youth Against Charges of Irresponsible Conduct." *United States Daily*, May 28, 1928, p. 2.

Published in part in "National Oratorical Contest." *Sojourner*, August 1928, pp. 9–10.

819 Address on accepting the Republican nomination for President of the United States, Palo Alto, California, August 11, 1928.

Published as Herbert Hoover's Acceptance Speech. Washington, D.C.: Republican National Committee, 1928. (Pamphlet.) "Address of Acceptance." In *Address of Acceptance . . .* (entry no. 14), part 1, and in *The New Day* (entry no. 15), pp. 7–44; "Address Accepting the Nomination." In *Public Papers*, 1929 (entry no. 51), pp. 499–520.

820 Address at West Branch, Iowa, August 21, 1928.

Published as Herbert Hoover Returns to Boyhood Scenes. Washington, D.C.: Republican National Committee, 1928. (Pamphlet.) "West Branch." In *The New Day* (entry no. 15), pp. 45–60, and in *Public Papers, 1929* (entry no. 51), pp. 521–529; "A Return to Boyhood Scenes." In *A Boyhood in Iowa* (entry no. 19), pp. 29–50.

821 Address at Newark, New Jersey, September 17, 1928.

Published as Herbert Hoover Champions Labor. Washington, D.C.: Republican National Committee, 1928. (Pamphlet.) "Newark, New Jersey." In *The New Day* (entry no. 15), pp. 61–86, and in *Public Papers, 1929* (entry no. 51), pp. 529–543.

822 Address at Elizabethton, Tennessee, October 6, 1928.

Published as Herbert Hoover and Campaign Issues. Washington, D.C.: Republican National Committee, 1928. (Pamphlet.) "Elizabethton, Tennesssee." In *The New Day* (entry no. 15), pp. 87–111, and in *Public Papers, 1929* (entry no. 51), pp. 543–557.

823   Address at Boston, Massachusetts, October 15, 1928.

Published as Address of Mr. Herbert Hoover Republican Nominee for President at Boston. (Pamphlet.) "Boston, Massachusetts." In *The New Day* (entry no. 15), pp. 113–145, and in *Public Papers, 1929* (entry no. 51), pp. 557–574.

824   Address at Madison Square Garden, New York City, October 22, 1928.

Published as "New York City." In *The New Day* (entry no. 15), pp. 147–176; and in *Public Papers, 1929* (entry no. 51), pp. 574–591.

Published in part as "Rugged Individualism." In *American Principles and Issues: The National Purpose*, edited by Oscar Handlin. New York: Holt, Rinehart and Winston, 1960, pp. 229–232.

825   Address at St. Louis, Missouri, November 2, 1928.

Published as Address of Mr. Herbert Hoover to Be Delivered at St. Louis, Missouri, Friday Evening.... N.p., n.d. (Pamphlet.) "St. Louis, Missouri." In *The New Day* (entry no. 15), pp. 177–208, and in *Public Papers, 1929* (entry no. 51), pp. 591–608.

826   Address by radio from Palo Alto, California, November 5, 1928.

Published as "Palo Alto, California." In *The New Day* (entry no. 15), pp. 209–215; "Radio Address to the Nation, Palo Alto, California." In *Public Papers, 1929* (entry no. 51), pp. 608–611.

827   Address at Amapala, Honduras, November 26, 1928.

Published as "Address of the Honorable Herbert Hoover . . . at the Custom House of Amapala. . . ." In *Addresses Delivered During the Visit to Central and South America* (entry no. 16), pp. 3–4; "Honduras." In *Public Papers, 1929* (entry no. 51), pp. 615–616.

828   Address at Cutuco, El Salvador, November 26, 1928.

Published as "Address of the Honorable Herbert Hoover . . . at Cutuco. . . ." In *Addresses Delivered During the Visit to Central and South America* (entry no. 16), p. 7; "El Salvador." In *Public Papers, 1929* (entry no. 51), pp. 618–619.

829   Address at Corinto, Nicaragua, November 27, 1928.

Published as "Address of the Honorable Herbert Hoover . . . on Board the U.S.S. Maryland, at Corinto. . . ." In *Addresses Delivered During the Visit to Central and South America* (entry no. 16), p. 9; "Nicaragua." In *Public Papers, 1929* (entry no. 51), pp. 620.

830   Address at San Jose, Costa Rica, November 28, 1928.

Published as "Address of the Honorable Herbert Hoover . . . at the National Theatre, San Jose. . . ." In *Addresses Delivered During the Visit to Central and South America* (entry no. 161), pp. 12–13; "Costa Rica." In *Public Papers, 1929* (entry no. 51), pp. 621–622.

831   Address at Guayaquil, Ecuador, December 1, 1928.

Published as "Address of the Honorable Herbert Hoover . . . at the Metropolitan Club, Guayaquil. . . ." In *Addresses Delivered During the Visit to Central and South America* (entry no. 16), pp. 16–17; "Ecuador." In *Public Papers, 1929* (entry no. 51), pp. 624–625.

832   Address at Lima, Peru, December 5, 1928.

Published as "Address of the Honorable Herbert Hoover . . . at the Government Palace, Lima. . . ." In *Addresses Delivered During the Visit to Central and South America* (entry no. 16), pp. 21–23; "Peru." In *Public Papers, 1929* (entry no. 51), pp. 626–629.

833   Address to Bolivia from Antofagasta, Chile, December 8, 1928.

Published as "Address of the Honorable Herbert Hoover . . . on Board the U.S.S. Maryland, Antofagasta, Chile. . . ." In *Addresses Delivered During the Visit to Central and South America* (entry no. 16), p. 26; "Bolivia." In *Public Papers, 1929* (entry no. 51), pp. 631–632.

834   Address at Santiago, Chile, December 11, 1928.

Published as "Address of the Honorable Herbert Hoover . . . at the Government Palace, Santiago. . . ." In *Addresses Delivered During the Visit to Central and South America* (entry no. 16), pp. 29–30; "Chile." In *Public Papers, 1929* (entry no. 51), pp. 633–635.

835 Address at Buenos Aires, Argentina, December 14, 1928.

Published as "Address of the Honorable Herbert Hoover . . . at the Government Palace, Buenos Aires. . . ." In *Addresses Delivered During the Visit to Central and South America* (entry no. 16), pp. 32–33; "Argentina." In *Public Papers, 1929* (entry no 51), pp. 636–638.

836 Address at Montevideo, Uruguay, December 17, 1928

Published as "Address of the Honorable Herbert Hoover . . . at the Parque Hotel, Montevideo. . . ." In *Addresses Delivered During the Visit to Central and South America* (entry no. 16), pp. 36–37; "Uruguay." *Public Papers, 1929* (entry no. 51), pp. 639–640.

837 Address at Montevideo, Uruguay, December 17, 1928.

Published as "Address of the Honorable Herbert Hoover . . . at the Palace of the National Administrative Council, Montevideo. . . ." In *Addresses Delivered During the Visit to Central and South America* (entry no. 16), p. 39; "Uruguay." In *Public Papers, 1929* (entry no. 51), p. 642.

838 Address at Rio de Janeiro, Brazil, December 22, 1928.

Published as "Address of the Honorable Herbert Hoover . . . at the Presidential Palace of Brazil, Rio de Janeiro. . . ." In *Addresses Delivered During the Visit to Central and South America* (entry no. 16), pp. 57–60; "Brazil." In *Public Papers, 1929* (entry no. 51), pp. 651–654.

839 Address before the Brazilian Congress, Rio de Janiero, Brazil, December 22, 1928.

Published as "Address of the Honorable Herbert Hoover . . . Before the Brazilian Congress, Rio de Janeiro. . . ." In *Addresses Delivered During the Visit to Central and South America* (entry no. 16), pp. 47–48; "Brazil." In *Public Papers, 1929* (entry no. 51), pp. 643–644.

840 Address before the Supreme Court of Brazil, Rio de Janeiro, Brazil, December 22, 1928.

Published as "Address of the Honorable Herbert Hoover . . . Before the Supreme Court of Brazil, Rio de Janeiro. . . ." In *Addresses Delivered During the Visit to Central and South America* (entry no. 16), p. 51; "Brazil." In *Public Papers, 1929* (entry no. 51), pp. 649–650.

1929

841 Address on his inauguration, Washington, D.C., March 4, 1929.

Published as "Inaugural Address. . . ." In *State Papers*, volume 1 (entry no. 45), pp. 3–12; "Inaugural Addresses." In *Public Papers, 1929* (entry no. 51), pp. 1–12.

Published in part as "Evil of Disregard for Law." In *Of Time and Truth*, edited by Fred W. Lorch and others. New York: Dryden Press, 1946, p. 508.

842 Address before the Gridiron Club, Washington, D.C., April 13, 1929.

Published as "Address Before the Gridiron Club . . . The Press and Public Opinion. Latin American Relations." In *State Papers*, volume 1 (entry no. 45), pp. 27–31; "Address to the Gridiron Club." In *Public Papers, 1929* (entry no. 51), pp. 67–72.

Published as part of "Addresses by President Hoover Before the Gridiron Club. . . ." In *Hoover After Dinner* (entry no. 21), pp. 3–12.

843 Address before the Associated Press, New York City, April 22, 1929.

Published as "Address at Annual Luncheon of the Associated Press . . . Respect for Law a National Duty." In *State Papers*, volume 1 (entry no. 45), pp. 42–47; "Address to the Associated Press: Law Enforcement and Respect for Law." In *Public Papers, 1929* (entry no. 51), pp. 101–106.

844 Address before the American Institute of Architects, Washington, D.C., April 25, 1929.

Published as "Washington, the City Beautiful." In *Development of the United States Capital: Addresses Delivered in the Auditorium of the United States Chamber of Commerce Building, Washington, D.C., at a Meeting Held to Discuss the Development of the National Capital, April 25, 1929.* 71st Congress, first session, 1930, House Document no. 35; "Address Before American Institute of Architects at Meeting on Development of the City of Washington. . . ." In *State Papers*, volume 1 (entry no. 45), pp. 47–49; "Address to the American Institute of Architects: Improvement of the National Capital." In *Public Papers, 1929* (entry no. 51), pp. 121–123.

845   Remarks on receiving the John Fritz Medal, Washington, D.C., April 25, 1929.

Published as "Remarks on Receiving the John Fritz Medal, Awarded by Engineering Organizations." In *Public Papers, 1929* (entry no. 51), pp. 123–124.

846   Remarks before the National Law Enforcement Commission, Washington, D.C., May 28, 1929.

Published as "Remarks at the Initial Meeting of the National Law *Enforcement Commission at the White House. . . ." In State Papers*, volume 1 (entry no. 45), pp. 63–64; "Remarks at the First Meeting of the National Commission on Law Observance and Enforcement." In *Public Papers, 1929* (entry no. 51), pp. 159–160.

847   Address on Memorial Day at Arlington National Cemetery, Arlington, Virginia, May 30, 1929.

Published as ". . . Armament Limitation Should Support Kellogg Pact." In *State Papers*, volume 1 (entry no. 45), pp. 64–67; "Memorial Day Address at Arlington National Cemetery." In *Public Papers, 1929* (entry no. 51), pp. 162–166.

848   Remarks at the cornerstone laying of the Department of Commerce Building, Washington, D.C., June 10, 1929.

Published as "Remarks at the Laying of the Corner Stone of the New Department of Commerce Building. . . ." In *State Papers*, volume 1 (entry no. 45), pp. 68–70; "Remarks Upon Laying the Cornerstone of the New Department of Commerce Building." In *Public Papers, 1929* (entry no. 51), pp. 180–181.

849   Remarks before the Federal Farm Board, Washington, D.C., July 15, 1929.

Published as "Remarks at the First Meeting of the Federal Farm Board . . . Responsibilities and Problems Before the Board." In *State Papers*, volume 1 (entry no. 45), p. 75; "Remarks at the First Meeting of the Federal Farm Board." In *Public Papers, 1929* (entry no. 51), pp. 220–221.

850   Address on the occasion of the Proclamation of the Treaty for the renunciation of war, Washington, D.C., July 24, 1929.

Published as "Address on the Occasion of the Proclamation of the General Pact for the Renunciation of War. . . ." In *State Papers*, volume 1 (entry no. 45), pp. 78–80; "Remarks Upon Proclaiming the Treaty for the Renunciation of War (Kellogg-Briand Pact)." In *Public Papers, 1929* (entry no. 51), pp. 233–235.

851   Remarks before the Planning Committee of the Proposed White House Conference on Child Health and Protection, Washington, D.C., July 29, 1929.

Published as "Remarks made . . . at the Initial Meeting of the Planning Committee of the Proposed White House Conference on Child Health and Protection." In *State Papers*, volume 1 (entry no. 45), pp. 83–84; "Remarks at the First Meeting of the White House Child Health Conference Planning Committee." In *Public Papers, 1929* (entry no. 51), pp. 238–239.

852   Address at Madison Courthouse, Virginia, August 17, 1929.

Published as "Address at Madison Courthouse, Virginia . . . Appreciation of the Rapidan Camp as a Week-end Relief. Response to the Welcome of the State of Virginia." In *State Papers*, volume 1 (entry no. 45), pp. 87–89.; "Remarks to the People of Madison County, Virginia, at the Celebration of Hoover Day in Madison."

In *Public Papers, 1929* (entry no. 51), pp. 255–257; "Address of President Hoover at Madison Courthouse." In *A Remedy for Disappearing Game Fishes* (entry no. 18), pp. 37–41.

853 Remarks on receiving Dr. Hugo Eckener at the White House, Washington, D.C., August 29, 1929.

Published as "Exchange of Remarks with Hugo Eckener, Commander of the Graf Zeppelin." In *Public Papers, 1929* (entry no. 51), pp. 271–272.

854 Address by radio from Washington, D.C., on occasion of the dedication of a new studio of station WABC, New York City, September 18, 1929.

Published as "Radio Address . . . Problems of Preparedness and Peace . . ." In *State Papers*, volume 1 (entry no. 45), pp. 100–102; "Radio Address to the Nation on Peace Efforts and Arms Reduction." In *Public Papers, 1929* (entry no. 51), pp. 294–295.

855 Remarks at Detroit, Michigan, October 21, 1929.

Published as "Remarks During a Motor Tour of Detroit, Michigan." In *Public Papers, 1929* (entry no. 51), p. 36.

856 Address on occasion of the fiftieth anniversary of the invention of the incandescent lamp, Dearborn, Michigan, October 21, 1929.

Published as "Mr. Hoover's Tribute to Mr. Edison." *Science* 70 (November 1, 1929):411–413; "Address at Dearborn, Michigan . . . at Celebration of the Fiftieth Anniversary of the Invention of the Incandescent Electric Lamp by Thomas A. Edison." In *State Papers*, volume 1 (entry no. 45), pp. 111–114; "Address on the Fiftieth Anniversary of Thomas Edison's Invention of the Incandescent Electric Lamp." In *Public Papers, 1929* (entry no. 51), pp. 337–340; "Address by President Hoover . . ." In *Hoover After Dinner* (entry no. 21), pp. 113–122.

857 Address on occasion of the completion of the Ohio River Development Project, Eden Park, Cincinnati, Ohio, October 22, 1929.

Published as ". . . Celebration of the Completion of the Ohio River Improvement Project." In *State Papers*, volume 1 (entry no. 45), pp. 114–116; "Remarks at Cincinnati, Ohio, Celebrating the Completion of the Ohio River Improvement Project." In *Public Papers, 1929* (entry no. 51), pp. 344–345.

858   Address on occasion of the completion of the Ohio River Improvement Project, Louisville, Kentucky, October 23, 1929.

Published as ". . . The Program of the Administration for the Development of Internal Waterways." In *State Papers*, volume 1 (entry no. 45), pp. 116–122; "Address at Louisville, Kentucky, Celebrating the Completion of the Ohio River Improvement Project." In *Public Papers, 1929* (entry no. 51), pp. 346–353.

859   Remarks at a ceremony honoring Madame Marie Curie, Washington, D.C., October 30, 1929.

Published as "Remarks at a Ceremony Honoring Madame Marie Curie." In *Public Papers, 1929* (entry no. 51), pp. 361–362.

860   Remarks on receiving South African Envoy, Eric Hendrik Louw, at the White House, Washington, D.C., November 5, 1929.

Published in "South African Envoy is Fourth Diplomat from British Empire." *United States Daily*, November 6, 1929, p. 3.

861   Address on Armistice Day, Washington, D.C., November 11, 1929.

Published as "Armistice Day Address . . . Preparedness for Peace and Immunity for Food Ships." In *State Papers*, volume 1 (entry no. 45), pp. 125–132; "Armistice Day Address." In *Public Papers, 1929* (entry no. 51), pp. 371–379.

862   Address before the Conference of Business Leaders of the United States Chamber of Commerce, Washington, D.C., December 5, 1929.

Published as ". . . Responsibility and Opportunity for Stabilization of Economic Welfare." In *State Papers*, volume 1 (entry no. 45), pp. 181–184; "Remarks to a Chamber of Commerce Conference on the Mobilization of Business and Industry for Economic Stabilization." In *Public Papers, 1929* (entry no. 51), pp. 453–455.

863 Address before the Gridiron Club, Washington, D.C., December 14, 1929.

Published as "Address before the Gridiron Club . . . The Use of Commissions and Committees." In *State Papers*, volume 1 (entry no. 45), pp. 187–193; "Address to the Gridiron Club." In *Public Papers, 1929* (entry no. 51), pp. 470–477.

Published as part of "Addresses by President Hoover Before the Gridiron Club. . . ." In *Hoover After Dinner* (entry no. 21, pp. 13–27.

1930

NOTE: At the time of compilation of this bibliography, *Public Papers* (entry no. 51) had been completed through 1929. As subsequent volumes in this series are published, *Public Papers* will be a major source for all presidential addresses.

864 Address by radio from Washington, D.C., to Community Chest workers, February 5, 1930.

Published as "Address to Community Chest Workers . . . Value of Community Chests and Appeal for Their Support." In *State Papers*, volume 1 (entry no. 45), p. 211.

865 Address on occasion of the twentieth anniversary of the founding of the Boy Scouts of America, Washington, D.C., March 10, 1930.

Published as "Address . . . at the Dinner Commemorating the Twentieth Anniversary of the Boy Scouts of America." In *State Papers*, volume 1 (entry no. 45), pp. 217–220; "An Address by President Hoover at the Dinner Commemorating the Twentieth Anniversary of the Boy Scouts of America. . . ." In *Hoover After Dinner* (entry no. 21), pp. 137–144.

866   Address at the dedication of the American Red Cross Building, Washington, D.C., March 19, 1930.

Published in "New Red Cross Home Dedicated by Mr. Hoover." *United States Daily*, March 20, 1930, p. 2.

867   Address at the birthday celebration of Dr. William H. Welch Washington, D.C., April 8, 1930.

Published as ". . . A Tribute to Dr. William H. Welch on Occasion of His Eightieth Birthday." In *State Papers*, volume 1 (entry no., 45), pp. 223–224.

868   Address on receiving the first Hoover Gold Medal at a dinner of the American Society of Mechanical Engineers, Washington, D.C., April 8, 1930.

Published as "Engineer's Opportunity in Public Service." *Mining and Metallurgy* 11 (May 1930):242; ". . . on Contribution Engineers Can Make to Public Service." In *State Papers*, volume 1 (entry no. 45), pp. 225–227.

869   Address before the Daughters of the American Revolution, Washington, D.C., April 14, 1930.

Published as ". . . Duty of the United States to Promote Peace in the World." In *State Papers*, volume 1 (entry no. 45), pp. 233–240.

870   Address before the American Society of Newspaper Editors, Washington, D.C., April 19, 1930.

Published as "Remarks to the American Society of Newspaper Editors." In *Public Papers, 1930* (entry no. 51), item no. 119. (This citation is from the galley proof of the 1930 volume.)

871   Address by radio from Washington, D.C., on the unveiling of the "Pioneer Woman" statue at Ponca City, Oklahoma, April 22, 1930.

Published as "Radio Broadcast . . . Tribute to Pioneer Women of the West." In *State Papers*, volume 1 (entry no. 45), pp. 243–244.

872 Address before the Gridiron Club, Washington, D.C., April 26, 1930.

Published as "... American Foreign Policy and Desire for Peace." In *State Papers*, volume 1 (entry no. 45), pp. 267–272.

Published as part of "Addresses by President Hoover Before the Gridiron Club...." In *Hoover After Dinner* (entry no. 21), pp. 29–40.

873 Address before the Chamber of Commerce of the United States, Washington, D.C., May 1, 1930.

Published as "... Certainty of Future Prosperity and Problems of Cooperation." In *State Papers*, volume 1 (entry no. 45), pp. 289–296.

874 Address before the American Red Cross, Washington, D.C., May 5, 1930.

Published as "... Expansion of the Activities and Influence of the Red Cross." In *State Papers*, volume 1 (entry no. 45), pp. 297–298.

875 Address at the opening of the Third National Conference on Street and Highway Safety, Washington, D.C., May 27, 1930.

Published as "... Great Loss of Human Life a Concern of National Importance." In *State Papers*, volume 1 (entry no. 45), pp. 300–302.

876 Address on Memorial Day, Gettysburg Battlefield, Pennsylvania, May 30, 1930.

Published as "Memorial Day Address ... Influence on our National Life of Ideals of Lincoln." In *State Papers*, volume 1 (entry no. 45), pp. 304–307.

877 Address at dinner in honor of President-elect Julio Prestes of Brazil, Washington, D.C., June 14, 1930.

Published in "The Governing Board Welcomes the President-Elect of Brazil, Dr. Julio Prestes." *Bulletin of the Pan American Union* 64 (August 1930):825–826.

878   Address on presenting the National Geographical Society Medal to Admiral Byrd, Washington, D.C., June 20, 1930.

Published as "Address . . . at the Presentation to Admiral Richard E. Byrd of the Special Gold Medal of the National Geographic Society." In *State Papers*, volume 1 (entry no. 45), pp. 318–319.

879   Address on the unveiling of a statue of James Buchanan, Washington, D.C., June 26, 1930.

Published in "President Hoover Lauds Career of James Buchanan." *United States Daily*, June 27, 1930, p. 2.

880   Address by radio from Washington, D.C., to the Governors' Conference, Salt Lake City, Utah, June 30, 1930.

Published as ". . . Appreciation of the Cooperation of the Governors of the States in Relief Construction. Summary of Work Accomplished." In *State Papers*, volume 1 (entry no. 45), pp. 345–347.

881   Address to welcome French aviators, Major Dieudonne Coste and Lt. Maurice Bellonte, Washington, D.C., September 8, 1930.

Published in "Progress of Man Based on Valor, President Says." *United States Daily*, September 9, 1930, p. 1.

882   Address before the Planning Committee of the President's Conference on Home Building and Home Ownership, Washington, D.C., September 24, 1930.

Published as ". . . The President's Statement to the Planning Committee of the Conference on Home Building and Home Ownership." In *State Papers*, volume 1 (entry no. 45), pp. 372–374.

883   Address before the American Bankers' Association, Cleveland, Ohio, October 2, 1930.

Published as ". . . Causes of the Present Depression and Possible Contribution of the Bankers Toward a Solution of the Problem." In *State Papers*, volume 1 (entry no. 45), pp. 375–384.

884 Address before the American Federation of Labor, Boston, Massachusetts, October 6, 1930.

Published as "Progress Toward Security and Stability." *Mining and Metallurgy* 11 (November 1930):508–509; ". . . Stability in Employment." In *State Papers*, volume 1 (entry no. 45), pp. 390–395.

885 Address before the American Legion, Boston, Massachusetts, October 6, 1930.

Published as ". . . The Promotion of Peace and Ideals of Citizenship." In *State Papers*, volume 1 (entry no. 45), pp. 384–390.

886 Address at King's Mountain Battlefield, South Carolina, October 7, 1930.

Published as "Address . . . in Celebration of the One Hundred and Fiftieth Anniversary of the Battle. The Principles and Ideals of American Life." In *State Papers*, volume 1 (entry no. 45), pp. 395–401.

887 Remarks at the Fifth International Oratorical Contest, Washington, D.C., October 25, 1930.

Published in "Oratorical Contests Helpful to Millions, President Declares." *United States Daily*, October 27, 1930, p. 2.

888 Address by radio from Washington, D.C., on occasion of the deposit of ratifications of the London Naval Treaty, October 27, 1930.

Published as ". . . World Broadcast on the Occasion of the Deposit of Ratifications of the London Naval Treaty." In *State Papers*, volume 1 (entry no. 45), pp. 406–407.

889 Address by radio from Washington, D.C., to the H. J. Heinz Company's International Radio Banquet, November 8, 1930.

Published in "President Says Industry Strife Proves Wasteful." *United States Daily*, November 10, 1930, p. 3.

Published as Remarks of President Hoover from the White House in Connection with the H. J. Heinz Company International Radio Banquet.... Washington, D.C.: Government Printing Office, 1930. (Pamphlet.)

890 Address before the Association of National Advertisers, Washington, D.C., November 10, 1930.

Published as "... Importance of Maintaining Public Confidence." In *State Papers*, volume 1 (entry no. 45), pp. 412–413.

891 Address on Armistice Day before the Annual Conference and Good-will Congress of World Alliance for International Friendship Through the Churches, Washington, D.C., November 11, 1930.

Published as "Armistice Day Address . . . The Obligation to Promote Peace and Prevent War." In *State Papers*, volume 1 (entry no. 45), pp. 413–417.

892 Address at the opening of the White House Conference on Child Health and Protection, Washington, D.C., November 19, 1930.

Published as "Child Health and Protection." *School and Society* 32 (November 29, 1930):711–715; "... The Safeguards and Services to Childhood." In *State Papers*, volume 1 (entry no. 45), pp. 419–426.

Published in part as "Forty-five Million Children." *Survey* 65 (December 15, 1930):313; "How to Stay Young." *This Week Magazine*, August 8, 1954, p. 2, and in *Addresses Upon the American Road, 1950–1955* (entry no. 38), p. 356.

893 Address by radio from Washington, D.C., to a 4-H Club Convention in Chicago, Illinois, December 2, 1930.

Published as "... Children Urged to Help in a Health Drive." In *State Papers*, volume 1 (entry no. 45), pp. 427–428.

894 Address before the Gridiron Club, Washington, D.C., December 13, 1930.

Published as "... Plea for Cooperation of Democratic Party and Protest Against Excessive Expenditures by Government." In *State Papers*, volume 1 (entry no. 45), pp. 466–471.

Published as part of "Addresses by President Hoover Before the Gridiron Club. ..." In *Hoover After Dinner* (entry no. 21), pp. 41–51.

1931

See note on page 125

895 Address by telephone from Washington, D.C., to the National Automobile Chamber of Commerce, New York City, January 6, 1931.

Published as "... No Need for Present Despondency." In *State Papers*, volume 1 (entry no. 45), pp. 477–478.

896 Address by radio from Washington, D.C., to appeal to the nation for contributions to the Red Cross, January 13, 1931.

Published as "Appeal to the Nation ... to Contribute At Least $10,000,000 to the Drought Relief Fund of the American Red Cross." In *State Papers*, volume 1 (entry no. 45), pp. 489–490.

897 Address by radio from Washington, D.C., to appeal to the nation for contributions to the Red Cross, January 22, 1931.

Published as "Radio Address from the White House ... Appeal to the Nation to Support the Red Cross Drive for $10,000,000 for Drought Relief." In *State Papers*, volume 1 (entry no. 45), p. 494.

898 Address by radio from Washington, D.C., on Lincoln's Birthday, February 12, 1931.

Published as "Radio Address on Lincoln's Birthday ... Dangers from Centralization and Bureaucracy to Liberty and Individual Initiative if National Government Assumes Local Relief." In *State Papers*, volume 1 (entry no. 45), pp. 500–505.

899   Address to the Puerto Rican Legislature, San Juan, Puerto Rico, March 24, 1931.

Published as "Address at San Juan . . . Encouragement in Economic Struggle and Pledge of Cooperation." In *State Papers*, volume 1 (entry no. 45), pp. 535–538.

900   Address on receiving the Belgian Ambassador, Paul May, at the White House, Washington, D.C., April 2, 1931.

Published in "Belgian Ambassador Presents Credentials to President Hoover." *United States Daily*, April 3, 1931, p. 3.

901   Address before the American Red Cross, Washington, D.C., April 13, 1931.

Published as ". . . Praise for Renewing and Invigorating Spiritual Life of the Nation." In *State Papers*, volume 1 (entry no. 45), pp. 540–542.

902   Remarks before the National Recreation Association Board of Directors Meeting, Washington, D.C., April 13, 1931.

Published as ". . . Recreation Vital to Public Health and Welfare." In *State Papers*, volume 1 (entry no. 45), pp. 542–543.

903   Address at Pan American Day Celebration, Washington, D.C., April 14, 1931.

Published as ". . . The Unity of Purpose and Ideals of the Republics of This Hemisphere." In *State Papers*, volume 1 (entry no. 45), pp. 543–545.

904   Address by radio from Washington, D.C., on occasion of the fiftieth anniversary of the Tuskegee Institute, Tuskegee, Alabama, April 14, 1931.

Published as ". . . The Contribution of Tuskegee to the Progress of the Negro Race." In *State Papers*, volume 1 (entry no. 45), pp. 545–547.

905   Address before the Gridiron Club, Washington, D.C., April 27, 1931.

Published as ". . . Meeting the Depression by Cooperation and Individual Effort." In *State Papers*, volume 1 (entry no. 45), pp. 554–558.

Published as part of "Addresses by President Hoover Before the Gridiron Club. . . ." In *Hoover After Dinner* (entry no. 21), pp. 53–63.

906 Address before the International Chamber of Commerce, Washington, D.C., May 4, 1931.

Published as ". . . Plea for Reduction of Armaments as Essential to Peace and Prosperity." In *State Papers*, volume 1 (entry no. 45), pp. 558–561.

907 Address at a celebration of the fiftieth anniversary of the American National Red Cross, Washington, D.C., May 21, 1931.

Published as ". . . The Spirit of the Organization." In *State Papers*, volume 1 (entry no. 45), pp. 563–565.

908 Address by radio from Washington, D.C., regarding the first annual meeting of the National Advisory Council on Radio in Education, May 22, 1931.

Published in "President Declares Speeches by Radio are Public Service." *United States Daily*, May 23, 1931, p. 3.

909 Address by radio from Camp Rapidan, Virginia, on the dedication of Cornell University's War Memorial, Ithaca, New York, May 23, 1931.

Published in "President Takes Part in Dedication of War Memorial." *United States Daily*, May 25, 1931, p. 2.

910 Address on Memorial Day, Valley Forge Park, Pennsylvania, May 30, 1931.

Published as ". . . The Source of Wisdom is in the People, Who Now Are Passing Through the Valley Forge of Depression." In *State Papers*, volume 1 (entry no. 45), pp. 565–570.

Published in part as "The Way to Greatness." *This Week Magazine*, February 23, 1958, p. 2.

911   Address before the Indiana Republican Editorial Association, Indianapolis, Indiana, June 15, 1931.

Published as "President Hoover's Plan." In *America Faces the Future*, edited by Charles A. Beard. New York: Houghton Mifflin Company, 1932, pp. 386–399; ". . . Business Depression and Policies of Government. The Remedy for Economic Depression Is Not Waste, But the Creation and Distribution of Wealth." In *State Papers*, volume 1 (entry no. 45), pp. 572–583.

Published in part as "A Twenty Year Plan for America." *Review of Reviews* 84 (July 1931):40–41.

912   Address at the dedication of the Harding Memorial, Marion, Ohio, June 16, 1931.

Published as ". . . Service and Tragedy in the Life of Warren G. Harding." In *State Papers*, volume 1 (entry no. 45), pp. 584–587.

913   Address at the dedication of the Lincoln Tomb, Springfield, Illinois, June 17, 1931.

Published as "Address at Springfield . . . A Product of the People, and the Symbol of the Union and of Human Rights." In *State Papers*, volume 1 (entry no. 45), pp. 587–590.

914   Address before a joint session of the Illinois Legislature, Springfield, Illinois, June 17, 1931.

Published as ". . .The State Legislatures Are Laboratories to Try Out New Ideas in Government." In *State Papers*, volume 1 (entry no. 45), pp. 590–591.

915   Remarks on welcoming Wiley Post and Harold Gatty to the White House, Washington, D.C., July 7, 1931.

Published in "President Hoover Commends Pilots for World Flight." *United States Daily*, July 7, 1931, p. 2.

916   Address by radio from Washington, D.C., to the Convention of International Christian Endeavor Societies, San Francisco, California, July 16, 1931.

Published as ". . . Praise for Aims and Accomplishments of the Societies." In *State Papers*, volume 1 (entry no. 45), pp. 599–600.

917 Address by radio from Camp Rapidan, Virginia, to World's Conference of Young Men's Christian Associations, Cleveland. Ohio, August 8, 1931.

Published as ". . . Work an Opportunity for Youth to Promote Common Good." In *State Papers*, volume 1 (entry no. 45), pp. 603–605.

918 Address by radio from Washington, D.C., on occasion of the fiftieth anniversary of the founding of the first Red Cross Chapter, September 9, 1931.

Published in "The President's Speech." *New York Times*, September 10, 1931, p. 2.

919 Address before the American Legion, Detroit, Michigan, September 21, 1931.

Published as ". . . Opposition to any Additional Governmental Expenditures Urged as Patriotic Service." In *State Papers*, volume 1 (entry no. 45), pp. 618–620.

Published in part as "America and World Recovery." *Review of Reviews* 84 (November 1931):68.

920 Address by radio from Washington, D.C., to the opening of the new Waldorf-Astoria Hotel, New York City, September 30, 1931.

Published in "Hotels Measure Nation's Growth, Says Mr. Hoover." *United States Daily*, October 1, 1931, p. 2.

Published in part in "A Home Away From Home" (entry no. 92), p. 1.

921 Address before the Pan American Commercial Conference, Washington, D.C., October 8, 1931.

Published as ". . . Nations Should Curb Non-Productive Spending." In *State Papers*, volume 2 (entry no. 45), pp. 7–9.

922 Address by radio from Washington, D.C., to a convention of the International Association of Chiefs of Police, St. Petersburg, Florida, October 12, 1931.

Published as ". . . Instead of Glorification of Gangsters We Should Have Glorification of Policemen Who Do Their Duty." In *State Papers*, volume 2 (entry no. 45), pp. 9–11.

923 Address by radio from Fortress Monroe, Virginia, October 18, 1931.

Published as Address of President Hoover on Unemployment Relief. Washington, D.C.: Government Printing Office, 1931. (Pamphlet.); ". . . Appeal for Voluntary Community Relief of the Unemployed." In *State Papers*, volume 2 (entry no. 45), pp. 12–15.

924 Address on occasion of the one-hundred and fiftieth anniversary of the surrender of Cornwallis, Yorktown, Virginia, October 19, 1931.

Published as ". . . Significance of Yorktown in American Ideas and Ideals." In *State Papers*, volume 2 (entry no. 45), pp. 15–18.

925 Address by radio from Washington, D.C., to the Methodist Ecumenical Congress, Atlanta, Georgia, October 25, 1931.

Published as ". . . A Plea for Cooperation Against War." In *State Papers*, volume 2 (entry no. 45), pp. 21–23.

926 Address by radio from Washington, D.C., to the National Broadcasters Association Convention, Detroit, Michigan, October 26, 1931.

Published in "Radio Regulation Preserves Free Speech, Says President." *United States Daily*, October 27, 1931, p. 1.

927 Address on Armistice Day, Washington, D.C., November 11, 1931.

Published as ". . . The Problem of the Establishment of World Peace." In *State Papers*, volume 2 (entry no. 45), pp. 28–30.

928 Address by radio from Washington, D.C., to a meeting of the Liberal Arts Colleges Association, November 14, 1931.

Published as "Liberal Arts Colleges." *School and Society* 34 (November 21, 1931):704; "... The Importance of these Colleges in Our Educational System." In *State Papers*, volume 2 (entry no. 45), pp. 35–36.

929 Address before the opening meeting of the President's Conference on Home Building and Home Ownership, Washington, D.C., December 2, 1931.

Published as "... The Problem of Home Ownership—Its Promotion and Protection." In *State Papers*, volume 2 (entry no. 45), pp. 36–40.

930 Address before the Gridiron Club, Washington, D.C., December 12, 1931.

Published as "... The President, the Political Party and the Press." In *State Papers*, volume 2 (entry no. 45), pp. 85–88.

Published as part of "Addresses by President Hoover Before the Gridiron Club...." In *Hoover After Dinner* (entry no. 21), pp. 65–72.

1932

See note on page 125

931 Address by radio from Washington, D.C., to the Lincoln Day Dinner of the National Republican Club, New York City, February 13, 1932.

Published as "... An Expression of Confidence in Our Popular Ability to Overcome Difficulty." In *State Papers*, volume 2 (entry no. 45), pp. 111–113.

932 Address before a joint session of Congress opening the celebration of the bicentennial of the birth of George Washington, Washington, D.C., February 22, 1932.

Published as ". . . Opening the Celebration of the Bicentennial of the Birth of George Washington." In *State Papers*, volume 2 (entry no. 45), pp. 119–125.

933   Address before the National Education Association, Mt. Vernon, Virginia, February 22, 1932.

Published as "Address of President Hoover at Mount Vernon." *School and Society* 35 (February 27, 1932):285; "Greetings." In *Addresses and Proceedings of the National Education Association of the United States*. N.p., 1932, p. 572.

934   Address by radio from Washington, D.C., on opening the anti-hoarding campaign, March 6, 1932.

Published as "Radio Address . . . on the Hoarding of Money." In *State Papers*, volume 2 (entry no. 45), pp. 137–139.

935   Address before the Gridiron Club, Washington, D.C., April 9, 1932.

Published as ". . . A Saving Sense of Humor and Patriotic Cooperation Are Needed in the Present Depression." In *State Papers*, volume 2 (entry no. 45), pp. 160–163.

Published as part of "Addresses by President Hoover Before the Gridiron Club. . . ." In *Hoover After Dinner* (entry no. 21), pp. 73–80.

936   Address before the Twenty-Fourth Conference of Governors, Richmond, Virginia, April 27, 1932.

Published as ". . . The Necessity for Reform in Taxation and in Governmental Expenditures." In *State Papers*, volume 2 (entry no. 45), pp. 169–175.

937   Address before the United States Senate, Washington, D.C., May 31, 1932.

Published as "Address to the United States Senate . . . Urging a Balanced Budget. . . ." In *State Papers*, volume 2 (entry no. 45), pp. 197–203.

938 Address at the commencement exercises of Howard University, Washington, D.C., June 10, 1932.

Published as ". . . Importance of Training Leaders of the Negro Race." In *State Papers*, volume 2 (entry no. 45), pp. 207–208.

939 Address on presenting the National Geographic Society Medal to Amelia Earhart, Washington, D.C., June 21, 1932.

Published in "Medal Presented by President to Amelia Earhart." *United States Daily*, June 22, 1932, p. 3.

940 Address on accepting the Republican nomination for president, Washington, D.C., August 11, 1932.

Published as ". . . Accepting the Republican Nomination for President. . . ." In *State Papers*, volume 2 (entry no. 45), pp. 247–265; "President Hoover, Acceptance Speech. . . ." In *Campaign Speeches of 1932* (entry no. 20), pp. 3–28.

941 Address on accepting on behalf of the government the Memorial Statue to Cardinal Gibbons, Washington, D.C., August 14, 1932.

Published as ". . . Accepting on Behalf of the Government the Memorial Statue to James, Cardinal Gibbons. . . ." In *State Papers*, volume 2 (entry no. 45), pp. 265–266.

942 Address before the Federal Reserve District Banking and Industrial Committees, Washington, D.C., August 26, 1932.

Published as ". . . Review of the Causes of Continued Depression and Suggestions for Remedial Aid." In *State Papers*, volume 2 (entry no. 45), pp. 268–274.

943 Address at the opening meeting of the Welfare Relief Mobilization Conference, Washington, D.C., September 15, 1932.

Published as ". . . Definite Tasks to Be Undertaken by Voluntary Agencies." In *State Papers*, volume 2 (entry no. 45), pp. 281–284.

944   Address at the cornerstone laying of the Post Office Department Building, Washington, D.C., September 26, 1932.

Published as ". . . The Growth and Importance of the Postal Service in American History." In *State Papers*, volume 2 (entry no. 45), pp. 285–287.

945   Address by radio from Washington, D.C., to the New York Herald Tribune's Women's Conference on Current Problems, New York City, September 29, 1932.

Published as ". . . The Ideals of the 'Children's Charter' to be Brought to Reality." In *State Papers*, volume 2 (entry no. 45), pp. 289–292; "President Hoover, New York Herald Tribune Conference. . . ." In *Campaign Speeches of 1932* (entry no. 20), pp. 279–283.

946   Address before delegates of the Republican Joint National Planning Committee to Get Out the Negro Vote, Washington, D.C., October 1, 1932.

Published as ". . . The Protection of Negro Rights is Pledged." In *State Papers*, volume 2 (entry no. 45), pp. 292–293.

947   Address at Des Moines, Iowa, October 4, 1932.

Published as "Campaign Speech . . . Agriculture." In *State Papers*, volume 2 (entry no. 45), pp. 293–318; "President Hoover, Des Moines, Iowa. . . ." In *Campaign Speeches of 1932* (entry no. 20), pp. 29–63.

948   Address at Fort Wayne, Indiana, October 5, 1932.

Published as "Campaign Speech . . . Campaign Falsehoods." In *State Papers*, volume 2 (entry no. 45), p. 319; "President Hoover, Fort Wayne. . . ." In *Campaign Speeches of 1932* (entry no. 20), pp. 64–65.

949   Address by radio from Washington, D.C., to women organizing support of the administration in the election campaign, October 7, 1932.

Published as "... Three Great Tasks Before the Nation." In *State Papers*, volume 2 (entry no. 45), pp. 320–328; "President Hoover, Women Voters. ..." In *Campaign Speeches of 1932* (entry no. 20), pp. 295–307.

950 Address before the American Bar Association, Washington, D.C., October 12, 1932.

Published as "... Lawyers Urged to Perform Duties of Citizenship." In *State Papers*, volume 2 (entry no. 45), pp. 328–335; "President Hoover, American Bar Association. ..." In *Campaign Speeches of 1932* (entry no. 20), pp. 284–294.

951 Address at Cleveland, Ohio, October 15, 1932.

Published as "Campaign Speech ... Unemployment and Wage and Salary Earners." In *State Papers*, volume 2 (entry no. 45), pp. 337–358; "President Hoover, Cleveland. ..." In *Campaign Speeches of 1932* (entry no. 20), pp. 80–109.

952 Address at Cumberland, Maryland, October 15, 1932.

Published as "Campaign Speech ... The Protective Tariff." In *State Papers*, volume 2 (entry no. 45), pp. 336–337; "President Hoover, Cumberland. ..." In *Campaign Speeches of 1932* (entry no. 20), pp. 308–309.

953 Address by radio from Washington, D.C., to appeal for community funds for relief, October 16, 1932.

Published as "... Appeal in Campaign for Community Funds for Relief During Winter of 1932–1933." In *State Papers*, volume 2 (entry no. 45), pp. 358–359.

954 Address at Charleston, West Virginia, October 22, 1932.

Published as "Campaign Speech ... Importance of the Protective Tariff to West Virginia." In *State Papers*, volume 2 (entry no. 45), pp. 359–364; "President Hoover, Charleston. ..." In *Campaign Speeches of 1932* (entry no. 20), pp. 313–319.

955   Address at Columbus, Ohio, October 22, 1932.

Published as "President Hoover, Columbus. . . ." In *Campaign Speeches of 1932* (entry no. 20), pp. 310–312.

956   Address at Detroit, Michigan, October 22, 1932.

Published as "Campaign Speech . . . Attack upon Statements of Democratic Candidate Concerning Government Finances and Review of Administration's Emergency Program." In *State Papers*, volume 2 (entry no. 45), pp. 364–384; "President Hoover, Detroit. . . ." In *Campaign Speeches of 1932* (entry no. 20), pp. 110–138.

957   Address before the American Public Health Association, Washington, D.C., October 24, 1932.

Published as ". . . Government Support to Local Health Units Is Advocated." In *State Papers*, volume 2 (entry no. 45), pp. 385–387; "President Hoover, American Public Health Association. . . ." In *Campaign Speeches of 1932* (entry no. 20), pp. 320–323.

958   Address at Indianapolis, Indiana, October 28, 1932.

Published as "Campaign Speech . . . Contrast of Administration Policies with Those of the Democratic Party and Candidates." In *State Papers*, volume 2 (entry no. 45), pp. 389–407; "President Hoover, Indianapolis. . . ." In *Campaign Speeches of 1932* (entry no. 20), pp. 139–166.

959   Address at Madison Square Garden, New York City, October 31, 1932.

Published as "Campaign Speech . . . The Campaign a Contrast Between Two Philosophies of Government. (Analysis of Democratic Proposals as Dangerous to the Foundations of American National Life.)" In *State Papers*, volume 2 (entry no. 45), pp. 408–428; "President Hoover, New York City. . . .." In *Campaign Speeches of 1932* (entry no. 20), pp. 167–196; "The Consequences of the Proposed New Deal." In *Addresses Upon the American Road, 1933–1938* (entry no. 24), pp. 1–19.

960 Address by radio and telephone from Washington, D.C., to political rallies in California, Oregon and Washington, November 2, 1932.

Published as "Text of President's Address by Telephone and Radio to West Coast." *New York Times,* November 3, 1932, p. 14.

961 Address at St. Louis, Missouri, November 4, 1932.

Published as "Campaign Speech ... The Democratic Campaign One of Avoidances (Account of the Dawes Bank Incident in Chicago and of the German Moratorium.)" In *State Papers,* volume 2 (entry no. 45), pp. 431–449; "President Hoover, St. Louis. . . ." In *Campaign Speeches of 1932* (entry no. 20), pp. 197–222.

962 Address at Springfield, Illinois, November 4, 1932.

Published in part in "President Hoover in Springfield Speech Reviews Events in Earlier History of Nation. . . ." *Commercial and Financial Chronicle* 135 (November 12, 1932):3266–3267.

963 Address at St. Paul, Minnesota, November 5, 1932.

Published as "Campaign Speech ... Importance of Economic Recovery (Administration Measures to Accomplish This, Compared with Democratic Policies Developed During the Campaign.)" In *State Papers,* volume 2 (entry no. 45), pp. 449–466; "President Hoover, St. Paul. . . ." In *Campaign Speeches of 1932* (entry no. 20), pp. 223–247.

964 Address at Denver, Colorado, November 6, 1932.

Published as "Text of President Hoover's Speech During His Stop at Denver." *New York Times,* November 7, 1932, p. 13.

965 Address at Salt Lake City, Utah, November 7, 1932.

Published as "Campaign Speech . . . Review of Republican Policies and Democratic Proposals (Special Reference to the Questions of Philippine Sugar, of Silver, and of the Futility of War)." In *State Papers,* volume 2 (entry no. 45), pp. 467–476; "President Hoover, Salt Lake City. . . ." In *Campaign Speeches of 1932* (entry no. 20), pp. 248–261.

966   Address by radio from Elko, Nevada, November 7, 1932.

Published as "Campaign Speech . . . Election Results Will Affect Welfare of Generations to Come." In *State Papers*, volume 2 (entry no. 45), pp. 476–479; "President Hoover, Elko. . . ." In *Campaign Speeches of 1932* (entry no. 20), pp. 269–273.

967   Address at San Francisco, California, November 8, 1932.

Published as "President Hoover, San Francisco. . . ." In *Campaign Speeches of 1932* (entry no. 20), pp. 324–325.

968   Address at Boulder Dam, Colorado, November 12, 1932.

Published as " .. . The Purposes of the Construction of Boulder Dam." In *State Papers*, volume 2 (entry no. 45), pp. 481–483; "President Hoover, Boulder Dam. . . ." In *Campaign Speeches of 1932* (entry no. 20), pp. 326–329.

969   Address at Glendale, California, November 12, 1932.

Published as ". . . Appeal to Republicans to Cooperate with the New Administration." In *State Papers*, volume 2 (entry no. 45), pp. 480–481; "President Hoover, Glendale. . . ." In *Campaign Speeches of 1932* (entry no. 20), pp. 274–275.

970   Address by radio from Washington, D.C., on opening   the Christmas Seal Campaign, November 25, 1932.

Published as "President Endorses Christmas Seals." *United States Daily*, November 28, 1932, p. 3.

971   Address before the Gridiron Club, Washington, D.C., December 10, 1932.

Published as ". . . Need for the Two Party System, but for Cooperation with the New Administration." In *State Papers*, volume 2 (entry no. 45), pp. 541–544.

Published as part of "Addresses by President Hoover Before the Gridiron Club. . . ." In *Hoover After Dinner* (entry no. 21), pp. 81–88.

972 Address of acceptance on behalf of the nation for the gift of Analostan Island as a memorial to Theodore Roosevelt, Washington, D.C., December 12, 1932.

Published as "... In Accepting in Behalf of the Nation the Gift of Analostan Island, as a Memorial to Theodore Roosevelt, from James R. Garfield, President of the Roosevelt Memorial Association." In *State Papers*, volume 2 (entry no. 45), p. 545.

973 Address at the cornerstone laying of the building for the Department of Labor and the Interstate Commerce Commission, Washington, D.C., December 15, 1932.

Published as "Address ... at the Laying of the Corner Stone of the Building for the Uses of the Department of Labor and the Interstate Commerce Commission. ..." In *State Papers*, volume 2 (entry no. 45), pp. 546–547.

1933

See note on page 125

974 Address at the opening of the Conference on the Crisis in Education, Washington, D.C., January 5, 1933.

Published as "... Proper Care and Training of Children More Important Than Any Other Process of Government." In *State Papers*, volume 2 (entry no. 45), pp. 564–565.

975 Address before the First Interstate Conference of Legislators, Washington, D.C., February 3, 1933.

Published as "... Urgent Need for Scientific Division of Tax Sources Amongst Governmental Authorities." In *State Papers*, volume 2 (entry no. 45), pp. 585–586.

976 Address at the Lincoln Day Dinner of the National Republican Club, New York City, February 13, 1933.

Published as "... International Cooperation Urged to Restore Economic Condition of World Recovery (Return to the Gold

Standard a Primary Step)." In *State Papers*, volume 2 (entry no. 45), pp. 586–595; "The Gold Standard and Recovery." In *Addresses Upon the American Road, 1933–1938* (entry no. 24), pp. 26–36.

977   Address at the cornerstone laying of the National Archives Building, Washington, D.C., February 20, 1933.

Published as "... The Records of Indissoluble Union." In *State Papers*, volume 2 (entry no. 45), p. 596.

978   Address at the cornerstone laying of the Department of Justice Building, Washington, D.C., February 23, 1933.

Published as "... Law the Foundation Stone of Organized Society." In *State Papers*, volume 2 (entry no. 45), pp. 599–600.

1934

979   Address before the Los Angeles Kiwanis Club, Los Angeles, California, September 5, 1934.

Published as "Address of Herbert Hoover." *Kiwanis Magazine* 19 (October 1934):448+.

1935

980   Address at the Lincoln Day Dinner of the National Republican Club, New York City, February 12, 1935.

Published in Addresses Delivered by Herbert Hoover, Harold B. Hoffman and Glenn Frank at the Forty-Ninth Annual Lincoln Dinner of the National Republican Club. ... New York: National Republican Club, 1935. (Pamphlet.)

981   Address before the California Republican Assembly, Sacramento, California, March 23, 1935.

Published as "Call to Republicans." *Vital Speeches* 1 (April 8, 1935):441–443; "Responsibility of the Republican Party to the Nation." In *Addresses Upon the American Road, 1933–1938* (entry no. 24), pp. 40–44.

982 Address at commencement exercises of Drake University, Des Moines, Iowa, June 3, 1935.

Published as Address by Herbert Hoover to the Graduating Class of Drake University.... (Des Moines, 1935). (Pamphlet.)

983 Address at commencement exercises of Stanford University, Palo Alto, California, June 16, 1935.

Published as The Essentials of Social Growth in America.... Stanford, California, 1935. (Pamphlet.) "Essentials of Economic and Social Security in America." In *Addresses Upon the American Road, 1933–1938* (entry no. 24), pp. 48–57.

984 Address at an Independence Day celebration, Grass Valley, California, July 4, 1935.

Published as Address... Independence Day Celebration, Grass Valley, California.... (Grass Valley, California, 1935). (Pamphlet.)

985 Address at a Constitution Day celebration, San Diego, California, September 17, 1935.

Published as "American Bill of Rights." *Vital Speeches* 2 (October 7, 1935):17–18; "The Bill of Rights." In *Addresses Upon the American Road, 1933–1938* (entry no. 24), pp. 58–62, and in *American Ideals Versus the New Deal* (entry no. 23), pp. 1–5.

986 Address before a conference of Republicans of eleven Western states, Oakland, California, October 5, 1935.

Published as "Printing Press Credit." *Vital Speeches* 2 (October 21, 1935):41–45; "Spending Deficits, Debts and Their Consequences." In *Addresses Upon the American Road, 1933–1938* (entry no. 24), pp. 63–74, and in *American Ideals Versus the New Deal* (entry no. 23), pp. 6–15.

987 Address before the Stanford University Alumni, New York City, October 10, 1935.

Published as "Address to Alumni of Stanford." *School and Society*

42 (October 19, 1935):546–547; *Address . . . before the Alumni of Stanford University. . . .* (New York, 1935). (Pamphlet.)

Published in part as "The Threat to Higher Learning." *Stanford Illustrated Review*, November 1935, p. 25.

988   Address before the Ohio Society of New York, New York City, November 16, 1935.

Published as "Criticism of the New Deal." *Vital Speeches* 2 (December 2, 1935):127–130; "The Consequences of 'Economic Planning' and Some Reforms It Requires." In *Addresses Upon the American Road, 1933–1938* (entry no. 24), pp. 75–86; "The Expenditures Imposed on the People by the New Economic Planning, Its Consequences, and Some Remedies It Requires." In *American Ideals Versus the New Deal* (entry no. 23), pp. 16–24.

989   Address before the John Marshall Republican Club, St. Louis, Missouri, December 16, 1935.

Published as "The Bank Panic and Relief Administration Reform." In *Addresses Upon the American Road, 1933–1938* (entry no. 24), pp. 87–100; "The New Deal Further Explored—With Special Reference to the Bank Panic and to Relief." In *American Ideals Versus the New Deal* (entry no. 23), pp. 25–35.

1936

990   Address before a Nebraska Republican Conference, Lincoln, Nebraska, January 16, 1936.

Published as "Freedom for the Farm." *Vital Speeches* 2 (January 27, 1936):271–275; "New Deal Agricultural Policies and Some Reforms." In *Addresses Upon the American Road, 1933–1938* (entry no. 24), pp. 101–103; "Further Explanations of the New Deal, Including Agricultural Policies." In *American Ideals Versus the New Deal* (entry no. 23), pp. 36–45.

991   Address at the Lincoln Day Dinner of the Multnomah County Republican Club, Portland, Oregon, February 12, 1936.

Published as "Tower of Babel." *Vital Speeches* 2 (February 24, 1936):332–335; "The Confused State of the Union." In *Addresses Upon the American Road, 1933–1938* (entry no. 24), pp. 114–125, and in *American Ideals Versus the New Deal* (entry no. 23), pp. 46–54.

992 Address before the Young Republican League of Colorado, Colorado Springs, Colorado, March 7, 1936.

Published as "True Liberalism in America." In *Addresses Upon the American Road, 1933–1938* (entry no. 24), pp. 126–141; "The Choice for Youth." In *American Ideals Versus the New Deal* (entry no. 23), pp. 55–65.

993 Address on occasion of the fifteenth anniversary of the Life Insurance Underwriters' Association, New York City, March 12, 1936.

Published as "The Trusteeship of Life Insurance." *Spectator*, March 19, 1936, p. 6+

994 Address at Fort Wayne, Indiana, April 4, 1936.

Published as "Effects of the New Deal." *Vital Speeches* 2 (April 20, 1936):444–449; "Are Our National Problems Being Solved?" In *Addresses Upon the American Road, 1933–1938* (entry no. 24), pp. 142–158; "Has the New Deal Solved Our National Problems?" In *American Ideals Versus the New Deal* (entry no. 23), pp. 66–78.

995 Address before the Republican Women of Pennsylvania, Philadelphia, Pennsylvania, May 14, 1936.

Published as "Constructive American Alternatives." *Vital Speeches* 2 (June 1, 1936):555–559; "An American Platform." In *Addresses Upon the American Road, 1933–1938* (entry no. 24), pp. 159–172; "The Obligations of the Republican Party to the American People." In *American Ideals Versus the New Deal* (entry no. 23), pp. 79–89.

996 Address before the Republican National Convention, Cleveland, Ohio, June 10, 1936.

Published as "Holy Crusade for Liberty." *Vital Speeches* 2 (June 15, 1936):570–573; "The Road to Freedom." In *Addresses Upon the American Road, 1933–1938* (entry no. 24), pp. 173–183; "Crisis to Free Men." In *American Ideals Versus the New Deal* (entry no. 23), pp. i–ix.

997 Address before the New York Herald Tribune Conference on Current Problems, New York City, September 23, 1936.

Published as "Relief." In *Report of the Sixth Annual New York Herald Tribune Forum on Current Problems.* New York: New York Herald Tribune, 1936, pp. 172–177; "Reform in the Administration of Relief." In *Addresses Upon the American Road, 1933–1938* (entry no. 24), pp. 186–192.

998 Address before the Metal Mining Congress, Denver, Colorado, September 30, 1936.

Published as "Reform in Some Federal Taxes." In *Addresses Upon the American Road, 1933–1938* (entry no. 24), pp. 193–200.

999 Address at a Republican rally, Philadelphia, Pennsylvania, October 16, 1936.

Published as "Book, Chapter and Verse." *Vital Speeches* 3 (November 2, 1936):49–53; "Intellectual Dishonesty in Government." In *Addresses Upon the American Road, 1933–1938* (entry no. 24), pp. 201–215.

1000 Address before the Young Republican League of Colorado, Denver, Colorado, October 30, 1936.

Published as "This Challenge to Liberty." In *Addresses Upon the American Road, 1933–1938* (entry no. 24), pp. 216–227.

1937

1001 Address before the Union League Club of Chicago, Chicago, Illinois, February 20, 1937.

Published as "This Is No Lawyer's Dispute Over Legalisms." *Vital Speeches* 3 (March 1, 1937):315–317; "Hands Off the Supreme Court." In *Addresses Upon the American Road, 1933–1938* (entry no. 24), pp. 229–236.

1002   Address before the annual convention of the Boys' Clubs of America, New York City, May 13, 1937.

Published as "The Business of Boys." In *Addresses Upon the American Road, 1933–1938* (entry no. 24), pp. 237–242.

1003   Address before the Massachusetts State Republican Club, Boston, Massachusetts, October 26, 1937.

Published as "New Blood in the Republican Party." *Vital Speeches* 4 (November 15, 1937):69–73; *Forward Motion of the Republican Party.* N.p., n.d. (Pamphlet.) "An Affirmative Program of American Ideals." In *Addresses Upon the American Road, 1933–1938* (entry no. 24), pp. 264–275.

1004   Address on occasion of the one-hundreth anniversary of the martyrdom of Elijah Parish Lovejoy, Colby College, Waterville, Maine, November 8, 1937.

Published as "Free Speech and Free Press." In *Addresses Upon the American Road, 1933–1938* (entry no. 24), pp. 276–280.

1005   Address at Syracuse University, Syracuse, New York, November 12, 1937.

Published as "Training for Public Service." In *Addresses Upon the American Road, 1933–1938* (entry no. 24), pp. 281–286.

1006   Address before the Economic Club of Chicago, Chicago, Illinois, December 16, 1937.

Published as "Lights Upon the Horizon." *Vital Speeches* 4 (January 1, 1938):186–189; "Economic Security and the Present Situation." In *Addresses Upon the American Road, 1933–1938* (entry no. 24), pp. 287–299.

1938

1007 Address before the Women's National Republican Club, San Francisco, California, January 15, 1938.

Published as "Former President Herbert Hoover's Peace Program." *Congressional Record*, 75th Congress, third session, 1938, 83, part 9:A236–238; "American Policies for Peace." In *Addresses Upon the American Road, 1933–1938* (entry no. 24), pp. 300–308.

1008 Address before the Council of Foreign Relations, New York City, March 31, 1938.

Published as "Greatest Service the Nation Can Give." *Vital Speeches* 4 (April 15, 1938):407–412; "The European Situation." *Congressional Record*. 75th Congress, third session, 1938, 83, part 10:A1528–1531; "Foreign Policies for America." In *Addresses Upon the American Road, 1933–1938* (entry no. 24), pp. 309–324.

1009 Address at a homecoming celebration, San Francisco, California, April 8, 1938.

Published as "Challenge to Liberty, 1938." In *Addresses Upon the American Road, 1933–1938* (entry no. 24), pp. 325–334.

1010 Address before the Modern Language Association of Central and Northern California, San Francisco, California, April 16, 1938.

Published as "Herbert Hoover on Foreign Languages." *Modern Language Journal* 22 (May 1938):646–647.

1011 Address before the California Council of Republican Women, Fresno, California, April 26, 1938.

Published as "Morals in Government." In *Addresses Upon the American Road, 1933–1938* (entry no. 24), pp. 335–342.

1012 Address at a Republican convention, Oklahoma City, Oklahoma, May 5, 1938.

Published as "It Is Our Blood." *Vital Speeches* 4 (June 1, 1938):

490–493; "The Dangerous Road for Democracy." In *Addresses Upon the American Road, 1933–1938* (entry no. 24), pp. 343–354.

1013 Address before the annual convention of the Boys' Clubs of America, Chicago, Illinois, May 19, 1938.

Published as The American Boy in a Democracy. New York: Boys' Clubs of America, 1938. (Pamphlet.) "Building Boys for America." In *Addresses Upon the American Road, 1933–1938* (entry no. 24), pp. 355–361.

Published in part as "Boys' Bill of Rights." *Scouting,* September 1938, p. 5.

1014 Address at the dedication of the Benjamin Franklin Institute, Philadelphia, Pennsylvania, May 21, 1938.

Published as "Franklin, A Characteristic American." *Vital Speeches* 4 (June 1, 1938):573–575; "On Benjamin Franklin." In *Addresses Upon the American Road, 1933–1938* (entry no. 24), pp. 362–368.

1015 Address before Republican delegations, Gallatin Gateway, Montana, August 6, 1938.

Published as Address at the Reception of Republican Delegations, Gallatin Gateway, Montana. N.p., 1938. (Pamphlet.)

1016 Address before Joint Republican Organizations, Kansas City, Missouri, September 28, 1938.

Published as "Morals in Government." *Vital Speeches* 5 (October 15, 1938):15–20; "Morals in Government." In *Further Addresses Upon the American Road, 1938–1940* (entry no. 28), pp. 3–20, and in *America's Way Forward* (entries no. 25 and 26), pp. 1–14.

1017 Address before Joint Republican Organizations, Hartford, Connecticut, October 17, 1938.

Published as "Undermining Representative Government." In *Further Addresses Upon the American Road, 1938–1940* (entry no. 28), pp. 21–28, and in *America's Way Forward* (entries no. 25 and 26), pp. 15–28.

1018 Address before the New York Herald Tribune Annual Forum on Current Problems, New York City, October 26, 1938.

Published as "America and the World Crisis." In *Further Addresses Upon the American Road, 1938–1940* (entry no. 28), pp. 85–92, and in *America's Way Forward* (entries no. 25 and 26), pp. 29–34.

1019 Address before the Joint Republican Organizations, Spokane, Washington, November 5, 1938.

Published as "The Economic Consequences of the New Deal." In *Further Addresses Upon the American Road, 1938–1940* (entry no. 28), pp. 39–57, and in *America's Way Forward* (entries no. 25 and 26), pp. 35–49.

1020 Address before the annual meeting of the York Bible Class, Toronto, Canada, November 22, 1938.

Published as "The Imperative Need for Moral Rearmament." In *Further Addresses Upon the American Road, 1938–1940* (entry no. 28), pp. 183–191, and in *America's Way Forward* (entry no. 26), pp. 50–56.

1939

1021 Address before the Council on Foreign Relations, Chicago, Illinois, February 1, 1939.

Published as "Our New Foreign Policy." *Vital Speeches* 5 (February 15, 1939):258–261; "President Roosevelt's New Foreign Policies." In *Further Addresses Upon the American Road, 1938–1940* (entry no. 28), pp. 93–103, and in *America's Way Forward* (entry no. 26), pp. 57–64; "New Departure in Our Foreign Policy." In *Shall We Send Our Boys to Foreign Wars?* (entry no. 27), pp. 3–5.

1022 Address before alumni of Stevens Institute of Technology, New York City, February 2, 1939.

Published as Devitalizing National Demons, issued by Stevens Institute of Technology. (Hoboken, New Jersey 1939). (Pamphlet.) "Engineers and Public Affairs." in *Further Addresses Upon the*

American Road, 1938–1940 (entry no. 28), pp. 192–196, and in *America's Way Forward* (entry no. 26), pp. 65–67.

1023 Address at the Lincoln Day Dinner of the National Republican Club, New York City, February 13, 1939.

Published as "The Real State of the Union." In *Further Addresses Upon the American Road, 1938–1940* (entry no. 28), pp. 58–68, and in *America's Way Forward* (entry no. 26), pp. 68–75.

1024 Address at Northwestern University, Evanston, Illinois, May 1, 1939.

Published as "Improving the Life of the Common Man." *Vital Speeches* 5 (May 15, 1939):453–454.

1025 Address at commencement exercises, Lincoln Memorial University, Harrowgate, Tennessee, June 4, 1939.

Published as "Compulsory Cooperation is Slavery." *Vital Speeches* 5 (June 15, 1939):514–517.; *The Clash of Economic Forces with Intellectual and Spiritual Liberty.* N.p. (1939). (Pamphlet.) "Your Inheritance of Liberty." In *Further Addresses Upon the American Road, 1938–1940* (entry no. 28), pp. 197–207.

1026 Address at commencement exercises, Earlham College, Richmond, Indiana, June 12, 1938.

Published as "Confusion in Words and Public Actions." *Earlhamite* (alumni magazine), July 1939, p. 3+; "And What Is Liberalism." In *Further Addresses Upon the American Road, 1938–1940* (entry no. 28), pp. 208–214.

1027 Address before the International Convention of Christian Endeavor Societies, Cleveland, Ohio, July 6, 1939.

Published as "A New Proposal For American Action." *Vital Speeches* 5 (July 15, 1939):582–584; "Let's Keep Women and Children Out of the Trenches." *Christian Herald*, August 1939, pp. 11–13+; "A New Proposal for American Action." In *Further Addresses Upon the American Road, 1938–1940* (entry no. 28), pp. 129–138, and in *Shall We Send Our Boys to Foreign Wars?* (entry no. 27), pp. 8–9.

1028　Address by radio from New York City, September 1, 1939.

Published as "War in Europe." *Vital Speeches* 5 (September 15, 1939): 736; *The Will to Keep Out of War.* San Francisco, California 1939). (Pamphlet.)

1029　Address on occasion of Pulaski Memorial Day, New York City, October 11, 1939.

Published as "The Spirit of Poland." In *Further Addresses Upon the American Road, 1938–1940* (entry no. 28), pp. 227–230.

1030　Address by radio from New York City, October 20, 1939.

Published as "The Arms Embargo." *Congressional Record.* 76th Congress, second session, 1939, 85, part 2:A497–498.

1031　Address before the Young Men's Christian Association Centennial Committee, New York City, November 2, 1939.

Published as "Prevent the Gangster of Tomorrow." *Sermons in Brief*, January 1940, pp. 57–59; "Address at Centennial Dinner of the YMCA." *School Review* 68 (March 1940):177–180.

1032　Address at Madison Square Garden, New York City, December 20, 1939.

Published as "Heroic Stand for Freedom." *Vital Speeches* 6 (January 15, 1940):219–220; *Helping Finland.* New York: Finnish Relief Fund, 1939. (Pamphlet.) "Relief of Finland." In *Further Addresses Upon the American Road, 1938–1940* (entry no. 28), pp. 231–235.

1940

1033　Address at the opening of the campaign of the Jewish Welfare Fund of Chicago, February 11, 1940, Chicago, Illinois.

Published as This Stricken World. . . . New York: American Jewish

Joint Distribution Committee, 1940. (Pamphlet.) "The Joint Distribution Committee Campaign of 1940." In *Further Addresses Upon the American Road, 1938–1940* (entry no. 28), pp. 241–245.

1034   Address before the Nebraska Republican Organizations, Omaha, Nebraska, February 12, 1940.

Published as "Our Most Important Domestic Issue." In *Further Addresses Upon the American Road, 1938–1490* (entry no. 28), pp. 69–84.

1035   Address at Madison Square Garden, New York City, March 12, 1940.

Published as "Relief for Poland." In *Further Addresses Upon the American Road, 1938–1940* (entry no. 28), pp. 246–249.

1036   Address at the dedication of the Madison Square Boys' Club, New York City, April 29, 1940.

Published as "A Boy's World." In *Further Addresses Upon the American Road, 1938–1940* (entry no. 28), pp. 219–226.

1037   Remarks at the dedication of the Belgian Pavilion at the World's Fair, New York City, May 18, 1940.

Published as "Belgian Pavilion at World's Fair." In *Addresses Upon the American Road, 1940–1941* (entry no. 29), p. 3.

1038   Address by radio from New York City, May 27, 1940.

Published as "Keep Politics Out of Our Defense Program." *Vital Speeches* 6 (June 15, 1940):520–523; "National Defense." In *Addresses Upon the American Road, 1940–1941* (entry no. 29), pp. 4–13.

1039   Address before the Republican National Convention, Philadelphia, Pennsylvania, June 25, 1940.

Published as "Republican National Convention." In *Addresses Upon the American Road, 1940–1941* (entry no. 29), pp. 205–223.

1040 Address at the University of Pennsylvania Symposium on Post-war Economic Problems, Philadelphia, Pennsylvania, September 18, 1940.

Published as "Our Future Economic Preparedness." *Vital Speeches* 7 (November 15, 1940):93–96; "Our Future Economic Defense." In *Studies in Economic and Industrial Relations*, by Wesley C. Mitchell and others. Philadelphia: University of Pennsylvania Press, 1941, pp. 25–36; "Our Future Economic Defense." In *Addresses Upon the American Road, 1940–1941* (entry no. 29), pp. 14–26.

1041 Address by radio from Columbus, Ohio, October 24, 1940.

Published as "The Third Term." In *Addresses Upon the American Road, 1940–1941* (entry no. 29), pp. 224–239.

1042 Address at Lincoln, Nebraska, October 31, 1940.

Published as "Our Foreign Relations." In *Addresses Upon the American Road, 1940–1941* (entry no. 29), pp. 34–51.

1043 Address at Salt Lake City, Utah, November 1, 1940.

Published as "The Major Issues." In *Addresses Upon the American Road, 1940–1941* (entry no. 29), pp. 240–255.

1044 Address at Poughkeepsie, New York, November 15, 1940.

Published as "America and the Famine in the Five Little Democracies." In *Addresses Upon the American Road, 1940–1941* (entry no. 29), pp. 121–131.

1045 Address by radio from the Metropolitan Opera House, New York City, December 7, 1940.

Published as "On American Liberty." In *Addresses Upon the American Road, 1940–1941* (entry no. 29), pp. 52–54.

1046 Address before the Pennsylvania Society of New York, New York City, December 21, 1940.

Published as "Problems that Confront Us." In *Vital Speeches* 7 (January 1, 1941):181–183; "Some National Problems." In *Addresses Upon the American Road, 1940–1941* (entry no. 29), pp. 55–62.

1941

1047 Address at Chicago, Illinois, February 16, 1941.

Published as "The March of Hunger in Europe" In *Addresses Upon the American Road, 1940–1941* (entry no. 29), pp. 147–155.

1048 Address before the Young Men's Christian Association, New Haven, Connecticut, March 28, 1941.

Published as "The Question of Peace." *Vital Speeches* 7 (April 15, 1941):405–408; "Our Part in Peace." *Congressional Record.* 77th Congress, first session, 1941, 87, part 11:A1493–1495; "The Question of Peace." In *Addresses Upon the American Road, 1940–1941* (entry no. 29), pp. 66–76.

1049 Address by radio from New York City, May 11, 1941.

Published as "We Are Not Prepared for War." *Vital Speeches* 7 (May 15, 1941):457–460; "The War Situation." *Congressional Record.* 77th Congress, first session, 1941, 87, part 11:A2228–2229; "The Immediate Relation of the United States to this War." In *Addresses Upon the American Road, 1940–1941* (entry no. 29), pp. 77–86.

1050 Address at commencement exercises, Haverford College, Haverford, Pennsylvania, June 7, 1941.

Published as "Commencement Exercises at Haverford College." In *Addresses Upon the American Road, 1940–1941* (entry no. 29), pp. 178–187.

Published in part as "Youth's Frontier Today." *Talks,* July 1941, pp. 26–28.

1051   Address on occasion of the fiftieth anniversary of Stanford University, Stanford, California, June 19, 1941.

Published as "Résumé." In *The University and the Future of America.* Stanford, California: Stanford University Press, 1941, pp. 267–274; "Address at the Symposium of the Fiftieth Anniversary of Stanford University." In *Addresses Upon the American Road, 1940–1941* (entry no. 29), pp. 188–195.

1052   Address at the dedication of the Hoover Library on War, Revolution and Peace, Stanford, California, June 20, 1941.

Published as "Dedication of the Hoover Library on War, Revolution and Peace." In *Addresses Upon the American Road, 1940–1941* (entry no. 29), pp. 196–198.

1053   Address by radio from Chicago, Illinois, June 29, 1941.

Published as "Call to Reason." *Vital Speeches* 7 (July 15, 1941): 580–584; "A Call to American Reason." In *Addresses Upon the American Road, 1940–1941* (entry no. 29), pp. 87–102; in *A Cause to Win* (entry no. 34), pp. 7–11; and in *Forty Key Questions* (entry no. 35), pp. 1–7.

1054   Address by radio from Chicago, Illinois, September 16, 1941.

Published as "Crisis." *Vital Speeches* 7 (October 1, 1941): 745–748; "The Crisis." In *Addresses Upon the American Road. 1940–1941* (entry no. 29), pp. 103–114.

1055   Address by radio from New York City, October 19, 1941.

Published as "Can Europe's Children Be Saved?" *Vital Speeches* 8 (November 15, 1941):68–71; "Can Europe's Children Be Saved?" In *Addresses Upon the American Road, 1955–1960* (entry no. 40), pp. 393–404.

1056   Address before the Union League Club of Chicago, Chicago, Illinois, November 19, 1941.

Published as "Shall We Send Armies to Europe?" *Vital Speeches* 8 (December 1, 1941):117–120.

1942

1057 Address before the annual convention of the Boys' Clubs of America, Chicago, Illinois, May 7, 1942.

Published as "Boys' Clubs in War." In *Addresses Upon the American Road, 1941–1954* (entry no. 31), pp. 375–377.

1058 Address before the National Industrial Conference Board, New York City, May 20, 1942.

Published as "The Limitations on Freedom in War." *Vital Speeches* 8 (June 1, 1942):487–489; "Address by Honorable Herbert Hoover on Dictatorial Rule During War." *Congressional Record.* 77th Congress, second session, 1942, 88, part 9:A1864–1866; "The Limitations on Freedom in War." In *Addresses Upon the American Road, 1941–1945* (entry no. 31), pp. 160–171.

1059 Address by radio from New York City, November 15, 1942.

Published as "In Spiritual Unity." *Talks*, January 1943, pp. 54–55; "United Church Canvass." In *Addresses Upon the American Road, 1941–1945* (entry no. 31), pp. 378–379.

1060 Address before the War Congress of American Industry, New York City, December 3, 1942.

Published as "Twelve Points to Guide Civilian Economy in Total War." *Time*, December 14, 1942, p. 30; "Some Principles of Civilian Economic Organization in Total War." In *Addresses Upon the American Road, 1941–1945* (entry no. 31), pp. 172–178.

1061 Address before the Executives' Club and other clubs, Chicago, Illinois, December 16, 1942.

Published as "New Approaches to Peace." *Vital Speeches* 9 (January 1, 1943):185–187; "The Approaches to Peace." In *Addresses Upon the American Road, 1491–1945* (entry no. 31), pp. 5–13.

1943

1062   Address at New York City, January 14, 1943.

Published as "Salvation Army Appeal." In *Addresses Upon the American Road, 1941–1945* (entry no. 31), pp. 380–381.

1063   Address before the National Industrial Conference Board, New York City, January 21, 1943.

Published as "Food Supplies for this War." In *Addresses Upon the American Road, 1941–1945* (entry no. 31), pp. 295–304.

1064   Address at Carnegie Hall, New York City, February 20, 1943.

Published as "Food for Europe's Children." In *Addresses Upon the American Road, 1941–1945* (entry no. 31), pp. 324–328.

1065   Address before the Midwest Governor's Conference, Des Moines, Iowa, March 15, 1943.

Published as "Our Food Front." In *Addresses Upon the American Road, 1941–1945* (entry no. 31), pp. 331–341.

1066   Address before the annual convention of the Boys' Clubs of America, New York City, May 6, 1943.

Published as "Boys' Clubs' Boys in the Army." In *Addresses Upon the American Road, 1941–1945* (entry no. 31), pp. 389–391.

1067   Address before the American Farm Bureau Federation, New York City, June 8, 1943.

Published as "Food Front." *Vital Speeches* 9 (June 15, 1943):535–528; "A Reform in Food Control." *Talks*, April 1943, pp. 25–27; "A Check Up on the Food Front." In *Addresses Upon the American Road, 1941–1945* (entry no. 31), pp. 342–352.

1068   Address by radio from New York City, July (?), 1943.

Published as "Africa—Sentimental Annex to Palestine." *Answer: War and Post-war Aims of the Jewish People*, August 1943, p. 14.

1069   Address before the joint session of the St. Paul–Minneapolis branches of the Foreign Policy Association and the University of Minnesota, Minneapolis, Minnesota, September 3, 1943.

Published as "New Approaches to Peace." *Vital Speeches* 10 (October 15, 1943):3–6; *Finding a Common Ground.* N.p., 1943, (Pamphlet.) "New Approaches to Peace." In *Addresses Upon the American Road, 1941–1945* (entry no. 31), pp. 71–84.

1070   Address at Kansas City, Missouri, October 28, 1943.

Published as "The Transition to Lasting Peace." In *Addresses Upon the American Road, 1941–1945* (entry no. 31), pp. 85–96.

1944

1071   Address before the annual convention of the Boys' Clubs of America, New York City, May 4, 1944.

Published as "The Need of Boys." In *Addresses Upon the American Road, 1941–1945* (entry no. 31), pp. 407–409.

1072   Address before the Republican National Convention, Chicago, Illinois, June 27, 1944.

Published as "Freedom in America and the World." In *Addresses Upon the American Road, 1941–1945* (entry no. 31), pp. 242–256.

1945

1073   Address before the Foreign Policy Association, Philadelphia, Pennsylvania, April 17, 1945.

Published as "The San Francisco Conference and Peace." *Vital Speeches* 11 (May 1, 1945):424–428; "The San Francisco Conference and Peace." in *Addresses Upon the American Road, 1941–1945* (entry no. 31), pp. 124–136.

1074   Address at Carnegie Hall, New York City, May 8, 1945.

Published as "Food for the Liberated Countries." In *Addresses Upon the American Road, 1941–1945* (entry no. 31), pp. 357–361.

1075   Address by radio from New York City, May 16, 1945.

Published as "On United States Army Taking Over Food Relief to the Liberated Countries of Western Europe." In *Addresses Upon the American Road, 1941–1945* (entry no. 31), pp. 362–364.

1076   Address before the Boys' Clubs of Chicago, Chicago, Illinois, June 6, 1945.

Published as "Chicago Boys' Club." In *Addresses Upon the American Road, 1941–1945* (entry no. 31), pp. 410–417.

1077   Address at San Francisco, California, July 18, 1945.

Published as "Progress Toward Enduring Peace." *Vital Speeches* 11 (August 15, 1945):646–647; "The San Francisco Charter and the Progress Toward Enduring Peace." In *Addresses Upon the American Road, 1941–1945* (entry no. 31), pp. 137–146.

1078   Address before the Iowa Association of Southern California, August 11, 1945.

Published as "The Challenge to Free Men." In *Addresses Upon The American Road, 1941–1945* (entry no. 31), pp. 257–264.

Published in Three Addresses by Herbert Hoover (entry no. 30), pp. 3–6.

1079   Address before the Executives' Club, Chicago, Illinois, September 17, 1945.

Published as "Post-war Foreign Loans." *Vital Speeches* 11 (October 1, 1945):750–753; "Postwar Foreign Loans." In *Addresses Upon the American Road, 1945–1948* (entry no. 32), pp. 3–13.

1080   Address before the North American Newspaper Alliance, New York City, September 27, 1945.

Published as "On Views on National Policies as to the Atomic Bomb." In *Addresses Upon the American Road, 1945–1948* (entry no. 32), pp. 14–15.

1081 Address on occasion of the fiftieth anniversary of Clarkson College of Technology, Potsdam, New York, October 8, 1945.

Published as "Economic Recovery from the War." In *Addresses Upon the American Road, 1945–1948* (entry no. 32), pp. 29–35;

Published in Three Addresses by Herbert Hoover (entry no. 30), pp. 7–11.

1082 Address on occasion of the seventy-fifth anniversary of Wilson College, Chambersburg, Pennsylvania, October 13, 1945.

Published as "The Uncommon Man." *Talks*, January 1946, pp. 11–13; "Moral and Spiritual Recovery from War." In *Addresses Upon the American Road, 1945–1948* (entry no. 32), pp. 36–43.

Published in Three Addresses by Herbert Hoover (entry no. 30), pp. 12–17.

1083 Address at the closing of the Yama Conference, Absecon, New Jersey, November 10, 1945.

Published as "An Extemporaneous Address Closing the Yama Conference of 1945." In *Addresses Upon the American Road, 1945–1948* (entry no. 32), pp. 44–48.

1084 Address by radio from New York City, November 10, 1945.

Published as "On the Twenty-fifth Anniversary of Radio." In *Addresses Upon the American Road, 1945–1948* (entry no. 32), pp. 141–145.

1946

1085 Address before the Lincoln Day dinner of the National Republican Club, New York City, February 12, 1946.

Published as "The Obligation of the Republican Party." In *Addresses Upon the American Road, 1945–1948* (entry no. 32), pp. 49–53.

1086 Address by radio from New York City, March 14, 1946.

Published as "On World Famine." In *Addresses Upon the American Road, 1945–1948* (entry no. 32), pp. 167–168.

1087 Address by radio from New York City, March 16, 1946.

Published as "On World Famine." In *Addresses Upon the American Road, 1945–1948* (entry no. 32), pp. 169–171.

1088 Address at Paris, France, March 21, 1946.

Published as "On World Famine Crisis." In *Addresses Upon the American Road, 1945–1948* (entry no. 32), pp. 172–173.

1089 Address at Rome, Italy, March 25, 1946.

Published as "On the Food Story of Italy." In *Addresses Upon the American Road, 1945–1948* (entry no. 32), pp. 174–175.

1090 Address by radio from Paris, France, March 27, 1946.

Published as "On the Food Situation in France." In *Addresses Upon the American Road, 1945–1948* (entry no. 32), pp. 176–178.

1091 Address at Prague, Czechoslovakia, March 28, 1946.

Published as "On Food Conditions in Czechoslovakia." In *Addresses Upon the American Road, 1945–1948* (entry no. 32), pp. 179–180.

1092 Remarks at a dinner given by President Bierut, Warsaw, Poland, March 29, 1946.

Published as "Remarks at Dinner of President Bierut." In *Addresses Upon the American Road, 1945–1948* (entry no. 32), pp. 181–182.

1093 Address at Warsaw, Poland, March 30, 1946.

Published as "On the Food Situation in Poland." In *Addresses Upon the American Road, 1945–1948* (entry no. 32), pp. 183–184.

1094 Address at Helsinki, Finland, April 1, 1946.

Published as "On Food Administration in Finland." In *Addresses Upon the American Road, 1945–1948* (entry no. 32), pp. 185–186.

1095 Address before the Emergency Conference on European Cereal Supplies, London, England, April 5, 1946.

Published as "Emergency Conference on European Cereal Supplies." In *Addresses Upon the American Road, 1945–1948* (entry no. 32), pp. 187–192.

1096 Address by radio from Cairo, Egypt, April 19, 1946.

Published as "Food Crisis." *Vital Speeches* 12 (May 1, 1946):420–421; "On the World Food Crisis." In *Addresses Upon the American Road, 1945–1948* (entry no. 32), pp. 193–198.

1097 Address by radio from Bombay, India, April 24, 1946.

Published as "On the World Food Situation." In *Addresses Upon the American Road, 1945–1948* (entry no. 32), pp. 199–202.

1098 Address at Bangalore, India, April 26, 1946.

Published as "On Food Difficulties in India." In *Addresses Upon the American Road, 1945–1948* (entry no. 32), pp. 203–205.

1099 Address at Manila, Philippines, April 29, 1946.

Published as "On the Food Problem in the Philippines." In *Addresses Upon the American Road, 1945–1948* (entry no. 32), p. 206.

1100 Address at Shanghai, China, May 3, 1946.

Published as "On the Food Needs of China." In *Addresses Upon the American Road, 1945–1948* (entry no. 32), p. 207.

1101 Address at Tokyo, Japan, May 6, 1946.

Published as "On the Japanese Food Supply." In *Addresses Upon the American Road, 1945–1948* (entry no. 32), p. 208.

1102 Address at San Francisco, California, May 10, 1946.

Published as "On the Effects of the Railroad Strike on World Famine." In *Addresses Upon the American Road, 1945–1948* (entry no. 32), pp. 209.

1103   Address by radio from Chicago, Illinois, May 17, 1946.

Published as "Hunger More Destructive Than Armies." *Vital Speeches* 12 (June 1, 1946):494–496; "History's Worst Famine." *Talks*, July 1946, pp. 3–6; "World Famine Situation." In *Addresses Upon the American Road, 1945–1948* (entry no. 32), pp. 221–228.

1104   Address before the Food and Agriculture Organization of the United Nations, Washington, D.C., May 20, 1946.

Published as "World Food Organization." *Congressional Record.* 79th Congress, second session, 1946, 92, part 11:A2785; "A New World Food Organization Needed." In *Addresses Upon the American Road, 1945–1948* (entry no. 32), pp. 229–231.

1105   Address in Mexico, May 28, 1946.

Published as "The Mission to Determine Needs of the Famine Areas." In *Addresses Upon the American Road, 1945–1948* (entry no. 32), pp. 233–234.

1106   Address at Bogotá, Colombia, May 31, 1946.

Published as "On World Famine." In *Addresses Upon the American Road, 1945–1948* (entry no. 32), pp. 235–236.

1107   Address at Quito, Ecuador, June 1, 1946.

Published as "On the Food Mission." In *Addresses Upon the American Road, 1945–1948* (entry no. 32), p. 237.

1108   Address at Lima, Peru, June 2, 1946.

Published as "On the World Famine Crisis." In *Addresses Upon the American Road, 1945–1948* (entry no. 32), pp. 238–244.

1109   Address at Santiago, Chile, June 5, 1946.

Published as "On the World Food Crisis." In *Addresses Upon the American Road, 1945–1948* (entry no. 32), pp. 245–251.

1110   Address at Buenos Aires, Argentina, June 10, 1946.

Published as "On World Food Crisis." In *Addresses Upon the American Road, 1945–1948* (entry no. 32), pp. 252–253.

1111 Address at Rio de Janeiro, Brazil, June 15, 1946.

Published as "On Communist Press Practices." In *Addresses Upon the American Road, 1945–1948* (entry no. 32), pp. 254–255.

1112 Address by radio from Ottawa, Canada, June 28, 1946.

Published as "Report on the World Famine." In *Addresses Upon the American Road, 1945–1948* (entry no. 32), pp. 259–266.

1113 Address at a banquet honoring the Prime Minister of Greece, Constantine Tsaldaris, New York City, December 16, 1946.

Published as "Address at a banquet In Honor of His Excellency, the Prime Minister of Greece." In *Addresses Upon the American Road, 1945–1948* (entry no. 32), pp. 267–268.

1947

1114 Remarks at the Greek War Relief Dinner, New York City, March 25, 1947.

Published as "On Greek Independence Day." In *Addresses Upon the American Road, 1945–1948* (entry no. 32), pp. 303–304.

1115 Address before the Gridiron Club, Washington, D.C., May 10, 1947.

Published as "Gridiron Dinner." In *Addresses Upon the American Road, 1945–1948* (entry no. 32), pp. 152–155.

1116 Address by radio from New York City, May 18, 1947.

Published as "A Pursuit of Happiness." *Talks*, July 1947, pp. 10–12.

1117 Address on occasion of the two-hundreth anniversary of Princeton University, Princeton, New Jersey, June 16, 1947.

Published as "In Celebration of Bicentennial Anniversary of

Princeton University." In *Addresses Upon the American Road, 1945–1948* (entry no. 32), pp. 156–162.

1118   Address at Madison Square Garden, New York City, September 21, 1947.

Published as "The World Food Situation." In *Addresses Upon the American Road, 1945–1948* (entry no. 32), pp. 306–310.

1119   Address before the Holland Society of New York, New York City, November 20, 1947.

Published as "Address Before the Holland Society of New York." In *Addresses Upon the American Road, 1945–1948* (entry no. 32), pp. 58–60.

1948

1120   Address at the Washington's Birthday Banquet of the Sons of the Revolution, New York City, February 23, 1948.

Published as "Address Before the Sons of the Revolution." In *Addresses Upon the American Road, 1945–1948* (entry no. 32), pp. 61–66.

1121   Address before the Republican National Convention, Philadelphia, Pennsylvania, June 22, 1948.

Published as "This Crisis in American Life." *Vital Speeches* 14 (June 1, 1948):548–550; "This Crisis in American Life." In *Addresses Upon the American Road, 1945–1948* (entry no. 32), pp. 67–73.

1122   Address at a homecoming birthday celebration, West Branch, Iowa, August 10, 1948.

Published as "The Meaning of America." *Vital Speeches* 14 (September 1948):674–676; "The Meaning of America." In *Addresses Upon the American Road, 1945–1948* (entry no. 32), pp. 74–82.

Published in part as "What We Mean by American." *Reader's Digest*, November 1948, pp. 81–84.

1123 Remarks by radio from New York City, October 11, 1948.

Published as "On Urging and Stimulating Voting." In *Addresses Upon the American Road, 1948–1950* (entry no. 33), p. 52.

1124 Remarks by telephone from New York City to Wilmington College, Ohio, November 11, 1948.

Published as "On the Uncommon Man." In *Addresses Upon the American Road, 1948–1950* (entry no. 33), pp. 171–172.

1949

1125 Address before the Economic Club of New York, New York City, January 26, 1949.

Published as "Federal Government Reorganization Will Save Billions." *Vital Speeches* 15 (February 15, 1949):261–262.

1126 Address before the Chamber of Commerce of New York State, New York City, March 3, 1949.

Published as "The Need for Reorganization." In *Addresses Upon the American Road, 1948–1950* (entry no. 33), pp. 142–145.

1127 Address at the Greater New York Funds Campaign Dinner, New York City, April 25, 1949.

Published as "The Government Can't Do It All." *This Week*, October 9, 1949, p. 5; "The Government Cannot Do It All." In *Addresses Upon the American Road, 1948–1950* (entry no. 33), pp. 174–176.

1128 Address at commencement exercises of the Institute for the Crippled and Disabled, New York City, June 6, 1949.

Published as "The Institute for the Crippled and Disabled." In *Addresses Upon the American Road, 1948–1950* (entry no. 33), pp. 177–178.

1129 Address at Ohio Wesleyan University, Delaware, Ohio, June 11, 1949.

Published as "Hoover Talk Urging Self-Reliance as Key to Progress." *Congressional Record.* 81st Congress, first session, 1949, 95, part 14:A3658–3659; "Give Us Self-reliance—or Give Us Security." In *Addresses Upon the American Road, 1948–1950* (entry no. 33), pp. 8–12.

Published in part as "What Is a Reactionary?" *Coronet*, February 1950, p. 51.

1130 Address at Stanford University, Stanford, California, August 10, 1949.

Published as "Think of the Next Generation." *Vital Speeches* 15 (September 1, 1949):676–678; "The Welfare State—Road to Collectivism." In *Great Political Thinkers*, by William Ebenstein. New York: Rinehart and Company, 1956, pp. 805–808; "Think of the Next Generation." In *Addresses Upon the American Road, 1948–1950* (entry no. 33), pp. 13–21.

1131 Address before the New York Board of Trade, New York City, October 18, 1949.

Published as "On Receiving an Award by New York Board of Trade." In *Addresses Upon the American Road, 1948–1950* (entry no. 33), pp. 55–58.

1132 Remarks before the Advertising Club, New York City, November 14, 1949.

Published as "On Advertising." In *Addresses Upon the American Road, 1948–1950* (entry no. 33), pp. 53–54.

1133 Address before the Citizen's Committee for the Hoover Reports, Washington, D.C., December 12, 1949.

Published as "Government Reforms Vital to Security." *Vital Speeches* 16 (January 1, 1950):169–171; "Removing Obstacles to Economy and to Competence in Government." In *Addresses Upon the American Road, 1948–1950* (entry no. 33), pp. 155–163.

1134   Address at New York City, December 14, 1949.

Published as "On the Salvation Army." In *Addresses Upon the American Road, 1948–1950* (entry no. 33), pp. 180–181.

1950

1135   Address before the Football Coach of the Year Dinner, New York City, January 12, 1950.

Published as "On Honoring the 1949 Football Coach of the Year." In *Addresses Upon the American Road, 1948–1950* (entry no. 33), pp. 182–184.

1136   Address on receiving the Moles' Award, New York City, February 9, 1950.

Published as "Engineering Society of the Moles." In *Addresses Upon the American Road, 1948–1950* (entry no. 33), pp. 187–190.

1137   Address by radio from New York City, March 11, 1950.

Published as "In Behalf of Boys' Clubs Week, 1950." In *Addresses Upon the American Road, 1948–1950* (entry no. 33), pp. 191–192.

1138   Address by telephone to a Salvation Army luncheon, Philadelphia, Pennsylvania, April 3, 1950.

Published as "Message to Salvation Army." In *Addresses Upon the American Road, 1948–1950* (entry no. 33), pp. 193–194.

1139   Address before the American Newspaper Publishers' Association, New York City, April 27, 1950.

Published as "The Voice of World Experience." *Vital Speeches* 16 (May 15, 1950):450–452; "The Voice of World Experience." In *Addresses Upon the American Road, 1948–1950* (entry no. 33), pp. 59–67, in *A Cause to Win* (entry no. 34), pp. 12–14, and in *Forty Key Questions* (entry no. 35), pp. 23–27.

1140   Address before the annual convention of the Boys' Clubs of America, Washington, D.C., May 18, 1950.

Published as "Pavement Boys." In *Addresses Upon the American Road, 1948–1950* (entry no. 33), pp. 195–199.

1141 Address before the United States Junior Chamber of Commerce, Chicago, Illinois, June 16, 1950.

Published as "Debts, Deficits and Taxes." In *Addresses Upon the American Road, 1948–1950* (entry no. 33), pp. 22–31.

1142 Remarks at the opening meeting of the Greater New York Fund Annual Campaign, New York City, June 1950.

Published as This Is Your Mission. Rochester, New York: Rochester Community Chest, 1950. (Pamphlet.)

1143 Address at the dedication of the William Allen White Memorial, Emporia, Kansas, July 11, 1950.

Published as "World Peace and the United Nations." *Vital Speeches* 16 (August 1, 1950):617–620; "The United Nations and World Peace." In *Addresses Upon the American Road, 1948–1950* (entry no. 33), pp. 68–77; "World Peace and the United Nations." In *A Cause to Win* (entry no. 34), pp. 15–20, and in *Forty Key Questions* (entry no. 35), pp. 31–40.

1144 Address by radio from New York City, October 19, 1950.

Published as part of "What Next in Foreign Policy." *U.S. News and World Report*, October 27, 1950, pp. 73–75.

Published as "Where We Are Now." *Vital Speeches* 17 (November 1, 1950): 37–39;"Where We Are Now." In *Addresses Upon the American Road, 1948–1950* (entry no. 33), pp. 91–99, and in *A Cause to Win* (entry no. 34), pp. 21–26; "Where Are We Now?" In *Forty Key Questions* (entry no. 35), pp. 43–53.

1145 Address on receiving the First Award of the Military Order of the Foreign Wars of the United States for Outstanding Citizenship, New York City, November 1, 1950.

Published as "When Disarmament Can Come." In *Addresses Upon the American Road, 1948–1950* (entry no. 33), pp. 100–106, and in *Forty Key Questions* (entry no. 35), pp. 57–62.

1146 Address by radio from New York City, December 20, 1950.

Published as "Our National Policies in This Crisis." *Vital Speeches* 17 (January 1, 1951):165–167; "Our National Policies in This Crisis." In *Addresses Upon the American Road, 1948–1950* (entry no. 33), pp. 203–210, in *A Cause to Win* (entry no. 34), pp. 27–32, and in *Forty Key Questions* (entry no. 35), pp. 65–74.

1951

1147 Address by radio from New York City, February 9, 1951.

Published as "We Should Revise Our Foreign Policies." *Vital Speeches* 17 (February 15, 1951):262–265; "We Should Revise Our Foreign Policies." In *Addresses Upon the American Road, 1950–1955* (entry no. 38), pp. 11–22.

Published in part as "Our Best Chance of Peace." *Reader's Digest*, April 1951, pp. 9–14.

1148 Remarks by radio from New York City, April 15, 1951.

Published as "A Discussion of *De Re Metallica*." In *Addresses Upon the American Road, 1950–1955* (entry no. 38), pp. 179–182.

1149 Address at the dedication of the Lighthouse for the Blind, New York City, April 25, 1951.

Published as "Dedication of the Lighthouse for the Blind." In *Addresses Upon the American Road, 1950–1955* (entry no. 38), pp. 282–283.

1150 Remarks before the American Newspaper Publishers Association, New York City, April 26, 1951.

Published as "Remarks." In *Addresses Upon the American Road, 1950–1955* (entry no. 38), p. 32.

1151 Address before the National Fund for Medical Education, New York City, May 16, 1951.

Published as "On Medical Education." In *Addresses Upon the American Road, 1950–1955* (entry no. 38), pp. 284-285.

1152 Address at the Iowa Centennial Celebration, Des Moines, Iowa, August 30, 1951.

Published as "Concerning Honor in Public Life." *Vital Speeches* 17 (September 15, 1951):716–718; "Concerning Honor in Public Life." In *Addresses Upon the American Road, 1950–1955* (entry no. 38), pp. 111–118.

1153 Address by radio from New York City, September 23, 1951.

Published as "On Behalf of Crusade for America." In *Addresses Upon the American Road, 1950–1955* (entry no. 38), pp. 33–34.

1154 Address at the dedication of the Herbert Hoover School, Kenmore, New York, October 10, 1951.

Published as "Dedication of the Herbert Hoover School." In *Addresses Upon the American Road, 1950–1955* (entry no. 38), pp. 312–315.

1155 Address before the Citizens Committee for the Hoover Reports, New York City, October 24, 1951.

Published as "Reorganization of the Government." In *Addresses Upon the American Road, 1950–1955* (entry no. 38), pp. 230–233.

1156 Address on receiving the Howard Coonley Gold Medal from the American Engineering Standards Association, New York City, October 24, 1951.

Published as "The Crusade for Standards." In *National Standards in a Modern Economy*, edited by Dickson Reck. New York: Harper and Brothers, 1956, pp. 3–4; "On Engineering Standards." In *Addresses Upon the American Road, 1950–1955* (entry no. 38), pp. 206–208.

1157 Address on launching the Columbia University Engineering Center Campaign Dinner, New York City, November 7, 1951.

Published as "Engineers." *Journal of Engineering Education* 43 (November 1952):133–135; "Engineers." In *Addresses Upon the American Road, 1950–1955* (entry no. 38), pp. 183–187.

1158 Address before the Mirror Youth Forum, New York City, December 1, 1951.

Published as "Address to Youth." In *Addresses Upon the American Road, 1950–1955* (entry no. 38), pp. 318–321.

1159 Address by radio from New York City, December 28, 1951.

Published as "On Reducing the Federal Wasteline." In *Addresses Upon the American Road, 1950–1955* (entry no. 38), pp. 234–236.

1160 Address by radio from New York City, December 1951.

Published as "This I Believe." In *Addresses Upon the American Road, 1950–1955* (entry no. 38), pp. 316–317.

1952

1161 Address by radio from New York City, January 27, 1952.

Published as "The Year Since the Great Debate." In *Addresses Upon the American Road, 1950–1955* (entry no. 38), pp. 35–44, and in *Forty Key Questions* (entry no. 35), pp. 91–102.

Published in part as "The Effective Military Policy for Us." *Reader's Digest*, May 1952, pp. 40–42.

1162 Address before the Second National Reorganization Conference of the Citizens Committee for the Hoover Reports, Washington, D.C., February 18, 1952.

Published as "Address by Herbert Hoover at the Second National Reorganization Conference. . . ." *Congressional Record*, 82nd Congress, second session, 1952, 98, part 1:1113–1114.

1163 Address at a dinner honoring Dr. Lee De Forest, New York City, April 8, 1952.

Published as "Address at Dinner Honoring Dr. Lee De Forest." In *Addresses Upon the American Road, 1950–1955* (entry no. 38), pp. 188–191.

1164   Address before the Gridiron Club, Washington, D.C., May 10, 1952.

Published as "Fishing Auguries." In *Addresses Upon the American Road, 1950–1955* (entry no. 38), pp. 323–327.

1165   Address before the Republican National Convention, Chicago, Illinois, July 8, 1952.

Published as "Freedom of Men." *Vital Speeches* 19 (November 1, 1952):43–47; "Address at Republican National Convention." In *Addresses Upon the American Road, 1950–1955* (entry no. 38), pp. 53–65.

1166   Address at the Northwest Engineering Centennial, Portland, Oregon, August 9, 1952.

Published as "On Engineers." In *Addresses Upon the American Road, 1950–1955* (entry no. 38), pp. 196–201.

1167   Address on occasion of the Centennial of Engineering, Chicago, Illinois, September 10, 1952.

Published as "The Scientists' and Engineers' Promise to American Life." In *Addresses Upon the American Road, 1950–1955* (entry no. 38), pp. 202–205.

1168   Address at the dedication of the San Francisco Boys' Club Building, San Francisco, California, September 25, 1952.

Published as "On Boys' Clubs." In *Addresses Upon the American Road, 1950–1955* (entry no. 38), pp. 286–290.

1169   Address by radio from New York City, October 18, 1952.

Published as "The Constructive Character of the Republican Party." In *Addresses Upon the American Road, 1950–1955* (entry no. 38), pp. 122–135.

1170   Address by radio from New York City, December 6, 1952.

Published as "On the Occasion of the Return of Freedom to Finland." In *Addresses Upon the American Road, 1950–1955* (entry no. 38), pp. 66–67.

1953

1171   Remarks before the Bohemian Club of San Francisco, San Francisco, California, March 19, 1953.

Published as "Remarks to the Bohemian Club of San Francisco." In *Addresses Upon the American Road, 1950–1955* (entry no. 38), pp. 334–336.

1172   Address on occasion of the Diamond Jubilee of Case Institute of Technology, Cleveland, Ohio, April 11, 1953.

Published as "Federal Socialization of Electric Power." *Vital Speeches* 19 (May 1, 1953):424–427; "Federal Socialization of Electric Power." In *Addresses Upon the American Road, 1950–1955* (entry no. 38), pp. 140–152.

1173   Address before the National Fund for Medical Education, New York City, April 16, 1953.

Published as "On the Problems of Medical Education." In *Addresses Upon the American Road, 1950–1955* (entry no. 38), pp. 295–296.

1174   Address at commencement exercises, Charlotte Hall Military Academy, Charlotte Hall, Maryland, June 1, 1953.

Published as "Commencement Exercises of Charlotte Hall Military Academy." In *Addresses Upon the American Road, 1950–1955* (entry no. 38), p. 338.

1175   Address at the dedication of the monument to powered flight, Pike's Peak, Colorado, August 26, 1953.

Published as "On the Dedication of the Monument to Powered Flight." In *Addresses Upon the American Road, 1950–1955* (entry no. 38), p. 341.

1176   Address on "Excursion," a television workshop, New York City, October 18, 1953.

Published as "Your Inheritance." In *Addresses Upon the American Road, 1950–1955* (entry no. 38), pp. 153–158.

1954

1177   Address before the International Benjamin Franklin Society, New York City, January 23, 1954.

Published as "Benjamin Franklin." *Vital Speeches* 20 (February 1, 1954):255–256; "Benjamin Franklin." In *Addresses Upon the American Road, 1950–1955* (entry no. 38), pp. 345–348.

1178   Remarks on occasion of Lincoln Day, Washington, D.C., February 5, 1954.

Published as "Lincoln Day Remarks." In *Addresses Upon the American Road, 1950–1955* (entry no. 38), p. 261.

1179   Address on receiving the American Good Government Society Award, by radio from Washington, D.C., February 22, 1954.

Published as "American Good Government Society Award." In *Addresses Upon the American Road, 1950–1955* (entry no. 38), pp. 159–162.

1180   Address before the National Press Club, Washington, D.C., March 10, 1954.

Published as "Outlook for Further Reorganization." In *Addresses Upon the American Road, 1950–1955* (entry no. 38), pp. 264–269.

1181   Address before the American Society of Newspaper Editors. Washington, D.C., April 17, 1954.

Published as "The Editors and the Federal Deficit." In *Addresses Upon the American Road, 1950–1955* (entry no. 38), pp. 163–170.

1182 Address on receiving the Economy Award at the Government Economy Rally of the Farm City Conference, New York City, May 25, 1954.

Published as "Farm City Conference Economy Award." In *Addresses Upon the American Road, 1950–1955* (entry no. 38), pp. 270–272.

1183 Address at Westown, Pennsylvania, May 29, 1954.

Published as "Address at the Westown School." In *Addresses Upon the American Road, 1950–1955* (entry no. 38), pp. 349–355.

1184 Address at the Hall of Fame Dinner, Chicago, Illinois, June 24, 1954.

Published as "Some National Problems." *Vital Speeches* 20 (August 15, 1954):650–652.

Published in part as "Some National Problems." In *Addresses Upon the American Road, 1950–1955* (entry no. 38), pp. 171–174; "On Foreign Policies." In *Addresses Upon the American Road, 1950–1955* (entry no. 38), pp. 70–73.

1185 Address at his eightieth birthday celebration, West Branch, Iowa, August 10, 1954.

Published as "United States Is Infected With Marxist Passion." *U.S. News and World Report*, August 20, 1954, pp. 103–104+; "Protection of Freedom." *Vital Speeches* 20 (September 1, 1954): 679–682; "The Philosophy of an American." *Congressional Record.* 84th Congress, first session, 1955, 101, part 18:A5042–5043; "Protection of Freedom." In *Addresses Upon the American Road, 1950–1955* (entry no. 38), pp. 74–84.

Published in part as "Herbert Hoover on Protection of Freedom." *Reader's Digest*, October 1954, pp. 144–148.

1186 Address at Washington, D.C., September 22, 1954.

Published as "On the Community Chest Drive." In *Addresses Upon the American Road, 1950–1955* (entry no. 38), pp. 298–300.

1187 Address before the West Side Association of Commerce of New York City, October 18, 1954.

Published as "On Reorganization of the Federal Government." In *Addresses Upon the American Road, 1955–1960* (entry no. 40), pp. 165–166.

1188 Address before the German and International Press Association, Bonn, Germany, November 24, 1954.

Published as "Some Hopes for Peace." In *Addresses Upon the American Road, 1950–1955* (entry no. 38), pp. 85–91, in *Speeches Delivered by Honorable Herbert Hoover in Germany* (entry no. 36), no. 1, and in *Three Addresses by Herbert Hoover in Germany* (entry no. 37), no. 1.

1189 Address on receiving an honorary degree from the University of Tubingen, Germany, November 25, 1954.

Published as "The Service of Universities." In *Addresses Upon the American Road, 1950–1955* (entry no. 38), pp. 92–96, in *Speeches Delivered by Honorable Herbert Hoover in Germany* (entry no. 36), no. 2, and in *Three Addresses by Herbert Hoover in Germany* (entry no. 37), no. 2.

1190 Address before the Municipal Senate of Berlin, Germany, November 26, 1954.

Published as "Resistance to Communism." In *Addresses Upon the American Road, 1950–1955* (entry no. 38), pp. 97–100, in *Speeches Delivered by Honorable Herbert Hoover in Germany* (entry no. 36), no. 3, and in *Three Addresses by Herbert Hoover in Germany* (entry no. 37), no. 3.

1955

1191 Address on receiving the Silver Quill Award of the National Business Publications, Washington, D.C., January 29, 1955.

Published as "On the Reorganization of the Federal Government." In *Addresses Upon the American Road, 1955–1960* (entry no. 40), pp. 167–171.

1192 Address before the United States Chamber of Commerce, Washington, D.C., May 4, 1955.

Published as "On Reorganization of the Federal Government." In *Addresses Upon the American Road, 1955–1960* (entry no. 40), pp. 172–176.

1193 Address before the National Industrial Conference Board, New York City, May 19, 1955.

Published as "The Work of the Commission on Reorganization of the Government." *Congressional Record.* 84th Congress, first session, 1955, 101, part 6:7701–7703; "On Reorganization of Federal Government." In *Addresses Upon the American Road, 1955–1960* (entry no. 40), pp. 177–185.

1194 Address at his eighty-first birthday celebration, Newburg, Oregon, August 10, 1955.

Published as "Our American Way of Life." In *Addresses Upon the American Road, 1955–1960* (entry no. 40), pp. 79–85.

Published in part as "Saying Something Good About Ourselves." *U.S. News and World Report,* August 19, 1955, p. 62; "Let's Say Something Good About Ourselves." *Reader's Digest,* February 1956, pp. 41–42.

1195 Address at the cornerstone laying of the building for the Columbia Boys' Clubs of San Francisco, San Francisco, California, August 28, 1955.

Published as "Here is the Cure of Delinquency and the Making of Good Citizens." In *Addresses Upon the American Road, 1955–1960* (entry no. 40), pp. 333–335.

1196 Remarks on accepting, on behalf of Herbert Hoover, Junior, the Gold Award of the New York Board of Trade, New York City, October 13, 1955.

Published as "On Herbert Hoover, Jr." In *Addresses Upon the American Road, 1955–1960* (entry no. 40), p. 369.

1197 Remarks on receiving the Frank H. Lahey Memorial Award from the National Fund for Medical Education, New York City, October 19, 1955.

Published as "Remarks on Receiving the Frank H. Lahey Memorial Award." In *Addresses Upon the American Road, 1955–1960* (entry no. 40), pp. 354–356.

1198 Address on presenting the West Side Association Gold Medal to Vice President Richard Nixon, New York City, October 27, 1955.

Published as "On the Vice Presidency." In *Addresses Upon the American Road, 1955–1960* (entry no. 40), pp. 215–217.

1199 Address by telephone for the dedication of the Herbert Hoover School, Tulsa, Oklahoma, November 8, 1955.

Published as "On Dedication of a School." In *Addresses Upon the American Road, 1955–1960* (entry no. 40), pp. 309–310.

1200 Address at the Tomb of the Unknown Soldier, Arlington National Cemetery, Arlington, Virginia, November 11, 1955.

Published as "At the Tomb of the Unknown Soldier." In *Addresses Upon the American Road, 1955–1960* (entry no. 40), pp. 86–87.

1956

1201 Remarks before the Citizens Committee for the Hoover Reports, Washington, D.C., January 16, 1956.

Published as "Statement to the Citizens' Committee for the Hoover Reports." In *Addresses Upon the American Road, 1955–1960* (entry no. 40), p. 231.

1202 Address before the United States Chamber of Commerce, Washington, D.C., March 15, 1956.

Published as "Reforms in the Civil Service and in Budgeting-Accounting." In *Addresses Upon the American Road, 1955–1960* (entry no. 40), pp. 236–244.

1203 Address before the Inter-American Bar Association, Dallas, Texas, April 16, 1956.

Published as "World Experience with the Karl Marx Way of Life." In *Addresses Upon the American Road, 1955–1960* (entry no. 40), pp. 16–26.

1204 Address before the United States Junior Chamber of Commerce, Washington, D.C., April 27, 1956.

Published as "Our Stake in Better Government." In *Addresses Upon the American Road, 1955–1960* (entry no. 40), pp. 245–247.

1205 Address on occasion of the fiftieth anniversary of the Boys' Clubs of America, New York City, May 10, 1956.

Published as "On Boys." In *Addresses Upon the American Road, 1955–1960* (entry no. 40), pp. 336–340.

1206 Address at the dedication of the Herbert Hoover Junior High School, San Francisco, California, June 5, 1956.

Published as "On the Shortage of Engineers." In *Addresses Upon the American Road, 1955–1960* (entry no. 40), pp. 280–283.

1207 Address at a Salvation Army luncheon, San Francisco, California, June 22, 1956.

Published as "On the Salvation Army." In *Addresses Upon the American Road, 1955–1960* (entry no. 40), pp. 358–359.

1208 Address before the Republican National Convention, San Francisco, California, August 21, 1956.

Published as "Herbert Hoover's Answer to 'America's Most Vital Issue'." *U.S. News and World Report,* August 31, 1956, pp. 70–71; "Address Before the Centennial Convention of the Republican Party." In *Addresses Upon the American Road, 1955–1960* (entry no. 40), pp. 93–98.

1209 Address at Cooper Union, New York City, October 9, 1956.

Published as "On Peter Cooper and Engineering." In *Addresses*

Upon the American Road, 1955–1960 (entry no. 40), pp. 284–285.

1210 Remarks at the cornerstone laying of the Union Oil Center, Los Angeles, California, October 17, 1956.

Published as "A Cornerstone Statement on Free Enterprise." In *Addresses Upon the American Road, 1955–1960* (entry no. 40), p. 100.

1211 Address by radio from New York City, October 29, 1956.

Published as "Reasons for Support of the Republican Party." In *Addresses Upon the American Road, 1955–1960* (entry no. 40), pp. 101–102.

1212 Address at the dedication of the General Robert E. Wood Boys' Club, Chicago, Illinois, November 19, 1956.

Published as "On General Robert Wood." In *Addresses Upon the American Road, 1955–1960* (entry no. 40), pp. 342–344.

1957

1213 Address before the Third National Reorganization Conference of the Citizens Committee for the Hoover Reports, Washington, D.C., February 4, 1957.

Published as "Inflation, Spending and Taxes." *Vital Speeches* 23 (March 1, 1957):313–314; "Inflation, Spending, Taxes and Some Reforms." *Congressional Record.* 85th Congress, first session, 1957, 103, part 2:1658–1659.

1214 Address by radio, February 7, 1957.

Published as "On the Hoover Institution on War, Revolution and Peace." In *Addresses Upon the American Road, 1955–1960* (entry no. 40), pp. 322–323.

1215 Remarks before the American Newspaper Publishers Association, New York City, April 25, 1957.

Published as "Remarks Before Annual Dinner of American Newspaper Publishers Association." In *Addresses Upon the American Road, 1955–1960* (entry no. 40), pp. 107–108.

1216　Address at commencement exercises, University of Southern California, Los Angeles, California, June 15, 1957.

Published as The Challenge of Tomorrow. N.p., 1957. (Pamphlet.)

1217　Address at the dedication of the Harry S. Truman Library, Independence, Missouri, July 6, 1957.

Published as "On the Truman Library." In *Addresses Upon the American Road, 1955–1960* (entry no. 40), p. 314.

1218　Address before the American Society of Newspaper Editors, San Francisco, California, July 1957.

Published as "On Inflation." In *Addresses Upon the American Road, 1955–1960* (entry no. 40), pp. 253–255.

1219　Remarks on occasion of his eight-third birthday on board the S.S. *President Hoover*, San Francisco, California, August 10, 1957.

Published as "On the S.S. *President Hoover*." In *Addresses Upon the American Road, 1955–1960* (entry no. 40), pp. 376–377.

1220　Address before the Grocery Manufacturers of America, New York City, November 11, 1957.

Published as "The Strengths of America." *Vital Speeches* 24 (December 15, 1957):154–155; "The Strengths of America." In *Addresses Upon the American Road, 1955–1960* (entry no. 40), pp. 111–113.

1221　Address before the United Engineering Society, New York City, November 21, 1957.

Published as "On Providing for a New Building for Our United Engineering Societies, and on the Reason and Cure for Our Great

National Shortage of Engineers and Scientists." In *Addresses Upon the American Road, 1955–1960* (entry no. 40), pp. 286–290.

1958

1222　Address on receiving an honorary Doctor of Laws from the Citadel State Military College, Charleston, South Carolina, January 13, 1958.

Published as "Upon Acceptance of an Honorary Degree." In *Addresses Upon the American Road, 1955–1960* (entry no. 40), pp. 378–382.

1223　Address at Freedom's Foundation, Valley Forge, Pennsylvania, February 22, 1958.

Published as "The Meaning of Valley Forge." In *Addressses Upon the American Road, 1955–1960* (entry no. 40), pp. 117–121.

1224　Address before the New York Chamber of Commerce, February 27, 1958.

Published as "Business Slumps and Recessions." *Vital Speeches* 24 (March 15, 1958):339–340; "Address by former President Hoover on Economic Recession." *Congressional Record*. 85th Congress, second session, 1958, 104, part 3:3195–3197; "Some Observations on Business Slumps and Recessions." In *Addresses Upon the American Road, 1955–1960* (entry no. 40), pp. 122–126.

1225　Address at the Brussels Exposition, Brussels, Belgium, July 4, 1958.

Published as "Invisible Forces Radiating from Nations." *Vital Speeches* 24 (August 1, 1958):619–621; "On American Ideals." In *Addresses Upon the American Road, 1955–1960* (entry no. 40), pp. 36–44, and in *Two Addresses in Brussels . . .* (entry no. 39), part 1.

1226　Address on occasion of Hoover Day, Brussels, Belgium, July 5, 1958.

Published as "On the Commission for the Relief of Belgium." In *Addresses Upon the American Road, 1955–1960* (entry no. 40), pp. 45–52, and in *Two Addresses in Brussels . . .* (entry no. 39), part 2.

1227 Address at the Institute of Nutrition Sciences, New York City, October 1, 1958.

Published as "On Nutrition." In *Addresses Upon the American Road, 1955–1960* (entry no. 40), pp. 128–129.

1228 Remarks on receiving a gold medal from the National Institute of Social Sciences, New York City, November 13, 1958.

Published as "Remarks at the Annual Dinner of the National Institute of Social Sciences." In *Addresses Upon the American Road, 1955–1960* (entry no. 40), pp. 291–292.

1229 Address at the dedication of the Dunlevy Milbank Children's Center, New York City, November 25, 1958.

Published as "On the Children's Aid Society." In *Addresses Upon the American Road, 1955–1960* (entry no. 40), pp. 364–366.

1230 Address before the Food Forum, New York City, November 1958.

Published as "On the Impact of Malnutrition on Civilization." In *Addresses Upon the American Road, 1955–1960* (entry no. 40), pp. 131–133.

1959

1231 Address on receiving the Hosea Ballou Medal, Tufts University, New York City, March 11, 1959.

Published as "On Acceptance of the Hosea Ballou Medal of Tufts University." In *Addresses Upon the American Road, 1955–1960* (entry no. 40), pp. 296–297.

1232 Address by radio, April 5, 1959.

Published as "Our Country's Crisis." *Congressional Record.* 86th Congress, first session, 1959, 105, part 20:A2968–2969; "This Crisis in the Principles and Morals in International Relations." In *Addresses Upon the American Road, 1955–1960* (entry no. 40), pp. 56–60.

1233   Address at the dedication of the Robert A. Taft Memorial, Washington, D.C., April 14, 1959.

Published as "Integrity and Courage." In *Addresses Upon the American Road, 1955–1960* (entry no. 40), pp. 134–137.

1234   Address at a dinner for the King of Belgium, New York City, May 28, 1959.

Published as "Address at Dinner for King of the Belgians." In *Addresses Upon the American Road, 1955–1960* (entry no. 40), pp. 61–63.

1235   Address at the cornerstone laying of School of Engineering Building, Cooper Union, New York City, September 17, 1959.

Published as "On the Cooper Union." In *Addresses Upon the American Road, 1955–1960* (entry no. 40), pp. 300–301.

1236   Remarks at the groundbreaking of the United Engineering Building, New York City, October 1, 1959.

Published as "Remarks at Groundbreaking Ceremonies of the United Engineering Building." In *Addresses Upon the American Road, 1955–1960* (entry no. 40), pp. 302–303.

1960

1237   Address before the National Council of United Presbyterian Men, New York City, February 13, 1960.

Published as "Current American Life: Some Observations." *Vital Speeches* 26 (March 15, 1960):324–325; "Some Observations on Current American Life." In *Addresses Upon the American Road, 1955–1960* (entry no. 40), pp. 149–154.

1238 Remarks before the American Newspaper Publishers Association, New York City, April 28, 1960.

Published as "Remarks Before the American Newspaper Publishers Association." In *Addresses Upon the American Road, 1955–1960* (entry no. 40), p. 155.

1239 Remarks at the cornerstone laying of the National Headquarters of the Boys' Clubs of America, New York City, May 1, 1960.

Published as "Remarks at the Cornerstone Laying of the National Headquarters of the Boys' Clubs of America." In *Addresses Upon the American Road, 1955–1960* (entry no. 40), pp. 349–350.

1240 Address before the annual convention of the Boys' Clubs of America, New York City, May 15, 1960.

Published as "On Boys' Clubs." In *Addresses Upon the American Road, 1955–1960* (entry no. 40), pp. 351–353.

1241 Address at the cornerstone laying of the United Engineering Center, New York City, June 16, 1960.

Published as "Address at Cornerstone Laying of United Engineering Center." In *Addresses Upon the American Road, 1955–1960* (entry no. 40), pp. 304–305.

1242 Address before the Republican National Convention, Chicago, Illinois, July 25, 1960.

Published as "Address at Republican National Convention. . . ." In *Addresses Upon the American Road, 1955–1960* (entry no. 40), pp. 156–161.

1961

1243 Address at the dedication of Herbert Hoover Dike, Lake Okeechobee, Florida, January 12, 1961.

Published as "Address by Herbert Hoover at the dedication of

Hoover Dike. . . ." *Congressional Record.* 87th Congress, first session, 1961, 107, part 1:1298–1299; *Dedication of the Herbert Hoover Dike.* N.p., 1961. (Pamphlet.)

1244   Address at Independence Hall, Philadelphia, Pennsylvania, June 27, 1961.

Published as "The Inheritance of the Next Generation." *Vital Speeches* 27 (August 1, 1961):631–632.

1962

1245   Address at the dedication of the Herbert Hoover Presidential Library, West Branch, Iowa, August 10, 1962.

Published as "Proposal for Greater Safety for America." *Vital Speeches* 28 (September 1, 1962):702–704; *Proposal for Greater Safety for America: The Assurance that We Are Not in the Decline and Fall of the American Way of Life.* N.p., 1962. (Pamphlet.)

Published in part as "From Herbert Hoover at Eighty-Eight: Words of Confidence and Hope." *U.S. News and World Report,* August 20, 1962, pp. 83–84.

Index: Subject

Index: Books and Collections